I KISSED DATING GOODBYE

JOSHUA HARRIS

I Kissed Dating Goodbye

MULTNOMAH BOOKS SISTERS, OREGON

I KISSED DATING GOODBYE
published by Multnomah Books
a part of the Questar publishing family

© 1997 by Joshua Harris
International Standard Book Number: 1-57673-036-0

Editor: Lisa Baba Lauffer
Copyeditor: Candace McMahan
Cover photo: Stephanie Rausser/FPG
Cover design: Kevin Keller
Back cover photograph: Nate Hilman

Printed in the United States of America

Unless otherwise indicated, all Bible quotations are from *The New International Version,* © 1973, 1984 by International Bible Society; used by permission of Zondervan Publishing House.

Also quoted:
The King James Version (KJV)

The New King James Version (NKJV) © 1984 by Thomas Nelson, Inc.

The Message: The New Testament in Contemporary Language © 1993 by NavPress; used by permission.

Scripture quotations marked (NLT) are taken from the *Holy Bible,* New Living Translation, © 1996. Used by permission of Tyndale House Publishers Inc., Wheaton, Illinois 60189. All rights reserved.

For information:
Questar Publishers, Inc.
Post Office Box 1720
Sisters, Oregon 97759

Library of Congress Cataloging-in-Publication Data:
Harris, Joshua.
    I kissed dating goodbye/by Joshua Harris. p.cm.
    Includes bibliographical references. ISBN 1-57673-036-0 (alk. paper) 1.
Dating (Social customs) 2. Dating (Social Customs)--Religious aspects--
Christianity. 3. Man-woman relationships. I.Title.
    HQ801.H329   1997   96-51843
    306.73--dc21   CIP
            98 99 00 01 02 03 04 — 11 10

To my parents, Gregg and Sono Harris.

Contents

Foreword

Hi.

Okay, I know what you're thinking. "I'll just skip these first few pages and get to the real stuff."

Well, hold on. Just wait. This foreword is preparation for what you are about to read.

Actually, that's exactly what this book is about—waiting and preparation. The ideas in these pages are really quite revolutionary. I'm so glad this book is in your hands; it could save you from a lot of needless agony. It has the potential to change the mind-set of our generation. It has already affected my life. Let me explain.

You see, for a long time, I have held the same kind of opinions on dating as Josh (the writer of this book and a friend of mine). I mean, as someone said to me recently, "Why shop if you're not gonna buy?" Exactly. Why date if you can't marry yet? I'm nineteen, and even though I've never dated, I've had plenty of years to watch some of my friends at the game. And believe me, it is a game. And it doesn't look fun. It looks agonizing and painful. That's part of the reason I haven't dated.

Second, I know it's not God's timing for me right now. I would just be distracted by having a boyfriend. Distracted from the work God wants me to do during these years.

I've also had the philosophy that groups and friendships are much more fun than one-on-one relationships at my age anyway.

But a little while ago I started to get a bit discouraged by the fact that I didn't have someone to get dressed up for and daydream about. That's when I read this book and really felt God encouraging me through Josh's words.

I don't think I've ever read a book in which the author is more honest and real than Josh is in this one. He tackles the hard issues, the tough questions on this confusing topic of "to date or not to date." And he gives practical answers. Joshua Harris has a powerful way of sharing from his experience. And since he's our age (just out of the teen years himself), he knows what he's talking about.

One of the things I like the most about Josh's writing is that he brings it all back to the Bible and how we can really live what it says. And after knowing him for the last couple of years, I can truly say that he "walks his talk."

So get ready to be challenged and encouraged, and prepare for your point of view to be taken on a ride!

Thanks for sticking with me and...enjoy.

Stay strong!
—Rebecca St. James

Introduction

Reading a book is a lot like a dating relationship. Granted, the analogy isn't perfect (you'd never take a book out to a movie), but when you read a book you do spend time alone. You hold it, stare into its face, and give it your undivided attention. Like a dating relationship, reading a book can carry you to the peaks and valleys of emotional experience—it can make you laugh or even make you angry.

I hope that you're not one of those "love 'em and leave 'em" types who read to the third chapter of a book and then dump it. If you are, you probably won't get much out of this one. As with a meaningful relationship, reading this book requires a certain level of commitment—a commitment to think hard and wrestle with ideas that will challenge your present views of dating.

Many wise people say that honesty is the best policy in any relationship. So before you "get serious" with this book, you need to understand one thing. This book isn't like other books on dating. Most other books will tell you how to fix dating to make it work for you. This book tells you how to "break up" with dating so your life works for God. *I Kissed Dating Goodbye* is about the reasons and ways to leave behind the world's lifestyle of dating.

Still want to go out?

WHAT I'M NOT GOING TO SAY

Maybe you're feeling a little nervous. "Kiss dating goodbye? Why would anyone choose not to date? How do you get married if you don't date? What about friendships? Get a life, buddy!"

I understand your hesitation, and we'll discuss all those things later in the book. But before we go any further, I want to state clearly what I'm *not* going to say about dating. I don't want you to spend your time worrying about what I might be implying. If you do, you'll miss the positive points and principles I intend to present.

I know this can happen because I've done it myself. When I was sixteen and in the middle of a two-year dating relationship, my mom gave me a copy of Elisabeth Elliot's book, *Passion & Purity*. I was immediately suspicious. Why? First, because my mom gave it to me. Giving me a book is my mom's not-so-subtle way of telling me I have a problem. Besides that, I was worried about the implications of the subtitle which read, "Bringing your love life under the authority of God." I was sure it was going to tell me that I wasn't allowed to kiss my girlfriend (something I thought very vital to my continued happiness at the time). So what did I do? I determined before I had even cracked the cover that I would disagree with everything the book had to say. As my mom likes to joke, I read all the "passion" but skipped all the "purity." What a mistake!

Not long ago I reread *Passion & Purity* and realized that, had I been more open-minded at the time, I could have benefited greatly from its message in the midst of my high school dating relationship. Why had it seemed so irrelevant? Why didn't I learn from it at that time? Because I had decided from the beginning that I wouldn't listen.

I hope you won't make the same mistake with this book. If you can remain open to this book's message, it may be exactly what you need to hear right now. To help you let down some of the defenses you may already have put up, let me make a couple of statements that should dispel two of the most common fears people have when I talk about giving up typical dating.

1. *I do not believe that dating is sinful.* Some people have sinned as a result of dating, but I don't think anyone can accurately say that dating in and of itself is a sinful activity. I view dating in a similar light as I view fast-food restaurants—it's not wrong to eat there, but something far better is available. As we'll see, God wants us to seek the best in everything, including our romantic relationships. As Christians, we're too often guilty of making do with the world's model for relationships and missing God's best.

2. *Rejecting typical dating does not mean that you'll never spend time alone with a guy or girl.* There's a difference between the act of going on a date and dating as a way of thinking about and approaching romantic relationships. If dating were merely a guy and girl going out for coffee, we wouldn't need to spend a whole book talking about it, would we? But dating is more than that. It's a lifestyle that involves our attitudes and values. And I want to encourage you to reexamine these patterns of thinking and acting.

I *won't* say that it's never appropriate to spend time alone with someone. At the right time in a relationship, if the motive is clear and the setting avoids temptation, going on a date can be healthy.

DATING ISN'T REALLY THE POINT

Having explained what I *won't* say in this book, let me tell you what I *will* say. In short, dating isn't really the point.

But, you ask, isn't this book *about* dating? And I can understand the question. After all (to extend the analogy between reading books and dating), you might have felt "attracted" to this book for any number of reasons—I'll list four:

1. You just got out of a bad relationship, and you don't want to be hurt again. Not dating sounds like a great idea.

2. You just haven't felt comfortable with dating, and you're looking for alternatives.

3. You're in a dating relationship that is headed in the wrong direction. You're looking for a way to keep the relationship within God's boundaries.

4. You're in a great dating relationship, and you're curious why anyone would choose not to date.

Can people coming from such different perspectives benefit from reading the same book? I believe they can. Why? Because, though their experiences with dating differ, they each have the same Creator. And our Creator's will and plan for our lives is the real focus of this book. Our ultimate purpose is not to figure out if Christians should date and, if so, how. Instead, as you read, I hope you look at the aspects of your life that dating touches—the way you treat others, the way you prepare for your future mate, your personal purity—and attempt to bring these areas into line with God's Word.

So even though in one sense this book is about dating, in another sense dating isn't really the point. The point is what God wants. Discussing if or how to date isn't an end in itself. Talking about it only serves a purpose when we view it in terms of its relation to God's overall plan for our lives.

You may or may not agree with some of the things I write. But if you stick around to read my case, if you at least walk away from this book with a more discerning spirit, my mission will have been accomplished, and your life could be enhanced. I hope that the ideas shared here will bring you a little closer to God's desire for your life.

I Kissed Dating Goodbye

CHAPTER ONE

Smart Love

BEYOND WHAT FEELS GOOD, BACK TO WHAT IS GOOD

It was finally here—Anna's wedding day, the day she had dreamed about and planned for months. The small, picturesque church was crowded with friends and family. Sunlight poured through the stained-glass windows, and the gentle music of a stringed quartet filled the air. Anna walked down the aisle toward David. Joy surged within her. This was the moment for which she had waited so long. He gently took her hand, and they turned toward the altar.

But as the minister began to lead Anna and David through their vows, the unthinkable happened. A girl stood up in the middle of the congregation, walked quietly to the altar, and took David's other hand. Another girl approached and stood next to the first, followed by another. Soon, a chain of six girls stood by him as he repeated his vows to Anna.

Anna felt her lip beginning to quiver as tears welled up in her eyes. "Is this some kind of joke?" she whispered to David.

"I'm…I'm sorry, Anna," he said, staring at the floor.

"Who are these girls, David? What is going on?" she gasped.

"They're girls from my past," he answered sadly. "Anna, they don't mean anything to me now…but I've given part of my heart to each of them."

"I thought your heart was mine," she said.

"It is, it is," he pleaded. "Everything that's left is yours."

A tear rolled down Anna's cheek. Then she woke up.

BETRAYED

Anna told me about her dream in a letter. "When I awoke I felt so betrayed," she wrote. "But then I was struck with this sickening thought: How many men could line up next to *me* on my wedding day? How many times have I given my heart away in short-term relationships? Will I have anything left to give my husband?"

I often think of Anna's dream. The jarring image haunts me. There are girls from my past, too. What if they showed up on my wedding day? What could they say in the receiving line?

"Hello, Joshua. Those were some pretty lofty promises you made at the altar today. I hope you're better at keeping promises now than you were when I knew you."

"My, don't you look nice in that tuxedo. And what a beautiful bride. Does she know about me? Have you told her all the sweet things you used to whisper in *my* ear?"

There are relationships that I can only look back on with regret. I do my best to forget. I laugh them off as part of the game of love that everyone plays. I know God has forgiven me because I've asked Him to. I know the various girls have forgiven me because I've asked them to.

But I still feel the ache of having given away my heart to too many girls in my past.

THAT'S JUST THE WAY IT IS

Growing up, I considered dating an essential part of the complete teenage experience. If I wasn't dating a girl, I had a crush on one.

This started in junior high when my peers and I treated dating as a game, a chance to play at love and experiment with relationships. Having a girlfriend meant little more than saying you were "going out." No big deal. My friends and I would go out with girls and break up with them at a frightening pace. The only worry was being dumped—you never wanted to *get* dumped, you wanted to *do* the dumping. One girl I knew had the fastest breakup routine ever: When she was ready to end a relationship, she'd say, "Skippy-bop, you just got dropped."

But soon, just saying you were going out with someone wasn't enough. Instead, we began experimenting with the physical side of relationships. Going out with someone came to mean you made out with that person, too. I remember standing by as a girl I liked called her boyfriend and broke up with him over the phone. As soon as she hung up, she kissed me. That meant we were an "official couple." Looking back, I can only shake my head at how immature we were. The physical intimacy of those junior high relationships had nothing to do with love or real affection. We just mimicked what we saw older kids do and what we watched in the movies. It seemed grown up, but in reality it was lust.

I'm thankful that junior high didn't last forever. In high school, I got serious about my walk with God and became actively involved in the church youth group. I put an "I'm Worth Waiting For" sticker on my NIV Student Bible and promised to stay a virgin until I got married. Unfortunately, youth group did little to improve my immature notions about relationships. Even in church we played the dating game with passion—more passion, I regret to say, than we gave to worshiping or listening to sermons. During Sunday morning services we passed notes about who liked whom, who was going out with whom, and who had broken up with whom.

Wednesday night youth group meetings served as our own opportunities to play "Love Connection," a game that resulted in broken hearts littering the foyer.

In my sophomore year, my involvement in the dating game took a more serious turn. That summer, I met Kelly. She was beautiful, blonde, and two inches taller than I. I didn't mind. Kelly was popular, and all the guys liked her. Since I was the only one in the youth group who had the nerve to talk to her, she wound up liking me. I asked her to be my girlfriend on the youth group's water ski retreat.

Kelly was my first serious girlfriend. Everyone in our youth group recognized us as a couple. We celebrated our "anniversary" every month. And Kelly knew me better than anyone else. After my folks were asleep, Kelly and I would spend hours on the phone, often late into the night, talking about everything and nothing in particular. We thought God had made us for each other. We talked about getting married someday. I promised her that I would love her forever.

But, like many high school relationships, our romance was premature—too much, too soon. We began to struggle with the physical side of our relationship. We knew we couldn't be as close physically as we were emotionally. As a result, we experienced ongoing tension, and it wore on us. Eventually, things turned sour.

"We have to break up," I said to her one night after a movie. We both knew this was coming.

"Is there any chance we can have something in the future?" she asked.

"No," I said, trying to add resolve to my voice. "No, it's over."

We broke up two years after we'd met. Not quite "forever," as I had promised.

SOMETHING BETTER

I was seventeen years old when my relationship with Kelly ended. My dreams of romance had ended in compromise, bitterness, and regret. I walked away asking, "Is this how it has to be?" I felt discouraged, confused, and desperate for an alternative to the cycle of short-term relationships in which I found myself. "God," I cried, "I want your best for my life! Give me something better than this!"

God answered that plea, but not in the way I had expected. I thought He'd bring me the ideal girlfriend or totally remove my desire for romance. Instead, He revealed through His Word what it meant to submit my love life to His Will—something I'd never truly done. I wanted God's best but hadn't been willing to play by His rules.

Over the past four years, I've come to understand that God's lordship doesn't merely tinker with my approach to romance—it completely transforms it. God not only wants me to act differently, He wants me to think differently—to view love, purity, and singleness from His perspective, to have a new lifestyle and attitude.

The basis of this new attitude is what I call "smart love." Paul describes this kind of love in Philippians 1:9–10:

> And this is my prayer: that your love may abound more and more in knowledge and depth of insight, so that you may be able to discern what is best and may be pure and blameless until the day of Christ.

Smart love constantly grows and deepens in its practical knowledge and insight; it opens our eyes to see God's best for our lives, enabling us to be pure and blameless in His sight.

SENTIMENTAL GUSH

The Message paraphrases Philippians 1:9–10 this way: "Learn to love appropriately. You need to use your head and test your feelings so that your love is sincere and intelligent, not sentimental gush."

Have you ever been guilty of "sentimental gush," allowing your emotions to dictate the course of a dating relationship? Many people do this. Instead of acting on what they know is right, couples let their feelings carry them away.

I've engaged in my share of sentimental gush. While dating, I made many decisions based on superficiality and ignorance. I could so easily say "I love you" to a girl, feigning selfless devotion, but in truth, selfishness and insincerity motivated me. I was primarily interested in what I could get, such as the popularity a girlfriend could give me or the comfort and pleasure I could gain physically or emotionally from a relationship. I didn't practice smart love. I lived "dumb love"—choosing what *felt* good for me instead of what *was* good for others and what pleased God.

To truly love someone with smart love, we need to use our heads as well as our hearts. As Paul describes it, love abounds in knowledge and insight. To "know" something is to understand or grasp it clearly and with certainty. "Insight" is an instance of understanding the true nature of something, the ability to see the motivation behind thoughts and actions.

With this definition in mind, let me ask you a few questions. Does love motivate the guy who sleeps with his girlfriend when it will scar her emotionally and damage her relationship with God? Does sincerity motivate the girl who leads a guy along then breaks up with him when she finds someone better? No! Both people exemplify selfish motivation. They need to "get smart" and realize how their actions affect others.

In recent years, I've tried to let sincere and intelligent love guide me, and as I've done this, I've come to some pretty intense conclusions for my life. I've come to realize that I have no business asking for a girl's heart and affections if I'm not ready to back up my request with a lifelong commitment. Until I can do that, I'd only be using that woman to meet *my* short-term needs, not seeking to bless *her* for the long term. Would I enjoy having a girlfriend right now? You bet! But with what I've learned as I've sought God's will for my life, I know that a relationship right now wouldn't be best for me or for the one I'd date. Instead, by avoiding romance before God tells me I'm ready for it, I can better serve girls as a friend, and I can remain free to keep my focus on the Lord.

KNOWING WHAT IS BEST

Waiting until I'm ready for commitment before pursuing romance is just one example of smart love in action. When our love grows in knowledge we can more readily "discern what is best" for our lives. Don't we all desperately need that discernment?

After all, when we engage in guy-girl relationships, we face some pretty hazy issues. Don't get me wrong—I believe in absolutes. But in dating, we don't only have to make wise choices between absolute wrong and absolute right. We also have to evaluate all parts of our dating relationships to make sure we don't go too far, allowing ourselves to get pulled into something we should avoid.

Here's an example. Let's say that someone at school asks you out. How do you seek guidance about what kind of person you can go out with? Try looking up "dating" in your Bible's concordance. You won't get far. Or maybe you've gone out on a few dates with someone, and you just kissed for the first time. It was exciting. You feel as if you're in love. But is it right?

How do we find answers to these questions? This is where "smart love" comes in. God wants us to seek guidance from scriptural truth, not feeling. Smart love looks beyond personal desires and the gratification of the moment. It looks at the big picture: serving others and glorifying God.

"What about me?" you might be asking. "What about my needs?" This is the awesome part: When we make God's glory and other people's needs our priority, we position ourselves to receive God's best in our lives as well. Let me explain.

In the past I made the starting point of my relationships what I wanted instead of what God wanted. I looked out for my needs and fit others into my agenda. Did I find fulfillment? No, I only found compromise and heartache. I not only hurt others, I hurt myself, and, most seriously, I sinned against God.

But when I reversed my attitude and made my main priority in relationships pleasing God and blessing others, I found true peace and joy. Smart love unlocks God's best for our lives. When I stopped viewing girls as potential girlfriends and started treating them as sisters in Christ, I discovered the richness of true friendship. When I stopped worrying about who I was going to marry and began to trust God's timing, I uncovered the incredible potential of serving God as a single. And when I stopped flirting with temptation in one-on-one dating relationships and started pursuing righteousness, I uncovered the peace and power that come from purity. I kissed dating good-bye because I found out that God has something better in store!

PURE AND BLAMELESS

The final benefit of seeking smart love is purity and blameless-ness before God. This purity goes beyond sexual purity. While physical purity is very important, God also wants us to pursue purity and blamelessness in our motives, our minds, and our emotions.

Does this mean we'll never mess up? Of course not! We can only stand before God because of His grace and the sacrifice of His Son, Jesus. And yet this grace doesn't give us license to be lax in our pursuit of righteousness. Instead, it should urge us to desire purity and blamelessness even more.

Ben started dating Alyssa during his senior year in college. For quite some time, he had planned to marry the summer after he graduated. Since he and Alyssa were both deeply attracted to each other, he thought she was "the one."

In a letter, Ben told me how he had grown up with very high standards in his dating relationships. Alyssa was another story. While Ben had never so much as kissed a girl, kissing was practically a sport for her. Unfortunately, Alyssa's values won out. "When she looked at me with those big brown eyes like I was depriving her of something, I caved in," Ben wrote. Their relationship soon became almost entirely physical. They maintained their virginity but only in the technical sense of the word.

A few months later, Alyssa began to be tutored in chemistry by another Christian guy whom Ben had never met. "That was a mistake," Ben wrote angrily. "They were studying chemistry all right—body chemistry!" Alyssa broke up with Ben and the next day was hanging on the arm of her new boyfriend.

"I was crushed," Ben told me. "I had violated my own standards, and more important, God's standards, and it turned out that this wasn't the woman I was to marry." For several months Ben wrestled with guilt but finally laid it at the foot of the cross and moved on, determined not to make the same mistake twice. But what about Alyssa? Yes, God can forgive her, too. But

I wonder if she ever realized she needs that forgiveness. When she passes Ben in the hall at school or sees him in the cafeteria, what goes through her mind? Does she realize she played a part in tearing down his purity? Does she feel pangs of guilt for breaking his heart? Does she even care?

I've shared with you how God has changed my perspective on dating. I've described how I've chosen to live my life and to interact with women until God shows me I'm ready for marriage. But why write a book about this perspective? What would make me think that anyone would want to hear what I have to say? Because I think God would like to challenge you, too.

I believe the time has come for Christians, male and female, to own up to the mess we've left behind in our selfish pursuit of short-term romance. Dating may seem an innocent game, but as I see it, we are sinning against each other. What excuse will we have when God asks us to account for our actions and attitudes in relationships? If God sees a sparrow fall (Matthew 10:29), do you think He could possibly overlook the broken hearts and scarred emotions we cause in relationships based on selfishness?

Everyone around us may be playing the dating game. But at the end of our lives, we won't answer to everyone. We'll answer to God. No one in my youth group knew how I compromised in my relationships. I was a leader and considered a good kid. But Christ says, "There is nothing concealed that will not be disclosed, or hidden that will not be made known" (Luke 12:2).

Our actions in relationships haven't escaped God's notice. But here's the good news: The God who sees all our sin is also ready to forgive all our sins if we repent and turn from them. He calls us to a new way of life. I know God has forgiven me for the sins I've committed against him and against the girl-friends I've had. I also know He wants me to spend the rest of my life living a lifestyle of smart love. The grace he has shown motivates me to make purity and blamelessness my passion.

I'm committed to practicing smart love, and I invite you along. Let's make purity and blamelessness our priority before our all-seeing, all-knowing God.

CHAPTER TWO

The Seven Habits of Highly Defective Dating

RECOGNIZING DATING'S NEGATIVE TENDENCIES

When I was a kid, my mom taught me two rules of grocery shopping. First, never shop when you're hungry—everything will look good and you'll spend too much money. And second, make sure to pick a good cart.

I've got the first rule down, but I haven't had much success with that second rule. I seem to have a knack for picking rusty grocery carts that make clattering noises or ones with squeaky wheels that grate on your nerves like fingernails on a chalkboard.

But by far the worst kind of cart you could pick is the "swerver." Have you ever dealt with one of these? This kind of cart has a mind of its own. You want to go in a straight line, but the cart wants to swerve to the left and take out the cat food display. (And, much to our dismay and embarrassment, it too often succeeds!) The shopper who has chosen a swerving cart can have no peace. Every maneuver, from turning down the cereal aisle to gliding alongside the meat section, becomes a battle—the shopper's will pitted against the cart's.

Why am I talking to you about shopping carts when this book is about dating? Well, I recall my bad luck with grocery carts because many times I've experienced a similar "battle of wills" with dating. I'm not talking about conflicts between me and the girls I've dated. I mean that I've struggled with the whole process. And based on my experiences and my exploration of God's Word, I've concluded that for Christians dating is a swerver—a set of values and attitudes that wants to go in a direction different from the one God has mapped out for us. Let me tell you why.

SELF-CONTROL ISN'T ENOUGH

I once heard a youth minister speak on the topic of love and sex. He told a heart-rending story about Eric and Jenny, two strong Christians who had actively participated in his youth group years earlier. Eric and Jenny's dating relationship had started out innocently—Friday nights at the movies and rounds of putt-putt golf. But as time went by, their physical relationship slowly began to accelerate, and they wound up sleeping together. Soon afterward they broke up, discouraged and hurt.

The pastor telling the story saw both of them years later at a high school reunion. Jenny was now married and had a child. Eric was still single. But both came to him separately and expressed emotional trauma and guilt over past memories.

"When I see him, I remember it all so vividly," Jenny cried.

Eric expressed similar feelings. "When I see her, the hurt comes back," he told his former youth pastor. "The wounds still haven't healed."

When the youth minister had finished telling this story, you could have heard a pin drop. We all sat waiting for some sort of solution. We knew the reality of the story he told. Some of us had made the same mistake or watched it happen in the lives of our friends. We wanted something better. We wanted the pastor to tell us what we were supposed to do instead.

But he gave no alternative that afternoon. Evidently the pastor thought the couple's only mistake was giving in to temptation. He seemed to think that Eric and Jenny should have had more respect for each other and more self-control. Although this pastor encouraged a different outcome—saving sex for marriage—he didn't offer a different practice.

Is this the answer? Head out on the same course as those who have fallen and hope that in the critical moment you'll be able to stay in control? Giving young people this kind of advice is like giving a person a cart that swerves and sending him into a store stocked with the world's most expensive Chinaware. Despite the narrow aisles and glass shelves laden with delicate dishes, this person is expected to navigate the rows with a cart known to go off course? I don't think so.

Yet this is exactly what we try in many of our relationships. We see the failed attempts around us, but we refuse to replace this "cart" called dating. We want to stay on the straight and narrow path and serve God, yet we continue a practice that often pull us in the wrong direction.

DEFECTIVE DATING

Dating has built-in problems, and if we continue to date according to the system as it is today, we'll more than likely swerve into trouble. Eric and Jenny probably had good intentions, but they founded their relationship on our culture's defective attitudes and patterns for romance. Unfortunately, even in their adulthood they continue to reap the consequences

The following "seven habits of highly defective dating" are some of the "swerves" dating relationships often make. Perhaps you can relate to one or two of them. (I know I can!)

1. *Dating leads to intimacy but not necessarily to commitment.*
Jayme was a junior in high school; her boyfriend, Troy, was a senior. Troy was everything Jayme ever wanted in a guy, and for eight months they were inseparable. But two months before Troy left for college, he abruptly announced that he didn't want to see Jayme anymore.

"When we broke up it was definitely the toughest thing that's ever happened to me," Jayme told me afterward. Even though they'd never physically gone beyond a kiss, Jayme had completely given her heart and emotions to Troy. Troy had enjoyed the intimacy while it served his needs but then rejected her when he was ready to move on.

Does Jayme's story sound familiar to you? Perhaps you've heard something similar from a friend, or maybe you've experienced it yourself. Like many dating relationships, Jayme and Troy's became intimate with little or no thought about commitment or how either of them would be affected when it ended. We can blame Troy for being a jerk, but let's ask ourselves a question. What's really the point of most dating relationships? Often dating encourages intimacy for the sake of intimacy— two people getting close to each other without any real intention of making a long-term commitment.

Deepening intimacy without defining a level of commitment is plainly dangerous. It's like going mountain climbing with a partner who isn't sure that she wants the responsibility of holding your rope. When you've climbed two thousand feet up a mountain face, you don't want to have a conversation about how she feels "tied down" by your relationship. In the same way, many people experience deep hurt when they open themselves up emotionally and physically only to be abandoned by others who proclaim they're not ready for "serious commitment."

An intimate relationship is a beautiful experience that God wants us to enjoy. But He has made the fulfillment of intimacy a byproduct of commitment-based love. You might say that intimacy between a man and a woman is the icing on the cake of a relationship headed toward marriage. And if we look at intimacy that way, then most dating relationships are pure icing. They usually lack a purpose or clear destination. In most cases, especially in high school, dating is short term, serving the needs of the moment. People date because they want to enjoy the emotional and even physical benefits of intimacy without the responsibility of real commitment.

In fact, that's what the original revolution of dating was all about. Dating hasn't been around forever. As I see it, dating is a product of our entertainment-driven, "disposable-everything" American culture. Long before *Seventeen* magazine ever gave teenagers tips on dating, people did things very differently.

At the turn of the twentieth century, a guy and girl became romantically involved only if they planned to marry. If a young man spent time at a girl's home, family and friends assumed that he intended to propose to her. But shifting attitudes in culture and the arrival of the automobile brought radical changes. The new "rules" allowed people to indulge in all the thrills of romantic love without having any intention of marriage. Author Beth Bailey documents these changes in a book whose title, *From Front Porch to Backseat,* says everything about the difference in society's attitude when dating became the norm. Love and romance became things people could enjoy solely for their recreational value.

Though much has changed since the 1920s, the tendency of dating relationships to move toward intimacy without commitment remains very much the same.

For Christians this negative swerve is at the root of dating's problems. Intimacy without commitment awakens desires—emotional and physical—that neither person can justly meet. In 1 Thessalonians 4:6 (KJV) the Bible calls this "defrauding," ripping someone off by raising expectations but not delivering on the promise. Pastor Stephen Olford describes defrauding as "arousing a hunger we cannot righteously satisfy"—promising something we cannot or will not provide.

Intimacy without commitment, like icing without cake, can be sweet, but it ends up making us sick.

2. Dating tends to skip the "friendship" stage of a relationship.

Jack met Libby on a church-sponsored college retreat. Libby was a friendly girl with a reputation for taking her relationship with God seriously. Jack and Libby wound up chatting during a game of volleyball and seemed to really hit it off. Jack wasn't interested in an intense relationship, but he wanted to get to know Libby better. Two days after the retreat he called her up and asked if she'd like to go out to a movie the next weekend. She said yes.

Did Jack make the right move? Well, he did in terms of scoring a date, but if he really wanted to build a friendship, he more than likely struck out. One-on-one dating has the tendency to move a guy and girl beyond friendship and toward romance too quickly.

Have you ever known someone who worried about dating a long-time friend? If you have, you've probably heard that person say something like this: "He asked me out, but I'm just afraid that if we start actually *dating* it will change our friendship." What is this person really saying? People who make statements like that, whether or not they realize it, recognize that dating encourages romantic expectations. In a true friendship you don't feel pressured by knowing you "like" the other person or that he or she "likes" you back. You feel free to be yourself and do things together without spending three hours in front of the mirror, making sure you look perfect.

C. S. Lewis describes friendship as two people walking side by side toward a common goal. Their mutual interest brings them together. Jack skipped this "commonality" stage by asking Libby out on a typical, no-brainer, dinner-and-movie date where their "coupleness" was the focus.

In dating, romantic attraction is often the relationship's cornerstone. The premise of dating is "I'm attracted to you; therefore, let's get to know each other." The premise of friendship, on the other hand, is "We're interested in the same things; let's enjoy these common interests together." If, after developing a friendship, romantic attraction forms, that's an added bonus.

Intimacy without commitment is defrauding. Intimacy without friendship is superficial. A relationship based only on physical attraction and romantic feelings will last only as long as the feelings last.

3. *Dating often mistakes a physical relationship for love.*
Dave and Heidi didn't mean to make out with each other on their first date. Really. Dave doesn't have "only one thing on his mind," and Heidi isn't "that kind of girl." It just happened. They had gone to a concert together and afterward watched a video at Heidi's house. During the movie, Heidi made a joke about Dave's attempt at dancing during the concert. He started tickling her. Their playful wrestling suddenly stopped when they found themselves staring into each other's eyes as Dave was leaning over her on the living room floor. They kissed. It was like something out of a movie. It felt so right.

It may have felt right, but the early introduction of physical affection to their relationship added confusion. Dave and Heidi hadn't really gotten to know each other, but suddenly they felt close. As the relationship progressed, they found it difficult to remain objective. Whenever they'd try to evaluate the merits of their relationship, they'd immediately picture the intimacy and passion of their physical relationship. "It's so obvious we love each other," Heidi thought. But did they? Just because lips have met doesn't mean hearts have joined. And just because two bodies are drawn to each other doesn't mean two people are right for each other. A physical relationship doesn't equal love.

When we consider that our culture as a whole regards the words "love" and "sex" as interchangeable, we shouldn't be surprised that many dating relationships mistake physical attraction and sexual intimacy for true love. Sadly, many Christian dating relationships reflect this false mind-set.

When we examine the progression of most relationships, we can clearly see how dating encourages this substitution. First, as we pointed out, dating does not always lead to lifelong commitment. For this reason, many dating relationships begin with physical attraction; the underlying attitude is that a person's primary value comes from the way he or she looks and performs as a date. Even before a kiss has been given, the physical, sensual aspect of the relationship has taken priority.

Next, the relationship often steamrolls toward intimacy. Because dating doesn't require commitment, the two people involved allow the needs and passions of the moment to take center stage. The couple doesn't look at each other as possible life partners or weigh the responsibilities of marriage. Instead, they focus on the demands of the present. And with that mind-set, the couple's physical relationship can easily become the focus.

And if a guy and girl skip the friendship stage of their relationship, lust often becomes the common interest that brings the couple together. As a result, they gauge the seriousness of their relationship by the level of their physical involvement. Two people who date each other want to feel that they're special to each other, and they can concretely express this through physical intimacy. They begin to distinguish their "special relationship" through hand holding, kissing, and everything else that follows. For this reason, most people believe that going out with someone means physical involvement.

Focusing on the physical is plainly sinful. God demands sexual purity. And He does this for our own good. Physical involvement can distort two people's perspective of each other and lead to unwise choices. God also knows we'll carry the memories of our past physical involvements into marriage. He doesn't want us to live with guilt and regret.

Physical involvement can make two people feel close. But if many people in dating relationships really examined the focus of their relationships, they'd probably discover that all they have in common is lust.

4. *Dating often isolates a couple from other vital relationships.*
While Garreth and Jenny were dating, they didn't need anyone else. Since it meant spending time with Jenny, Garreth had no problem giving up Wednesday night Bible study with the guys. Jenny didn't think twice about how little she talked to her younger sister and mother now that she was dating Garreth. Nor did she realize that when she did talk to them, she always started her sentences with "Garreth this…" and "Garreth said such and such…" Without intending to, both had foolishly and selfishly cut themselves off from other relationships.

By its very definition, dating is about two people focusing on each other. Unfortunately, in most cases the rest of the world fades into the background. If you've ever felt like a third wheel hanging out with two friends who are dating each other, you know how true this is.

Granted, of all dating's problems, this one is probably the easiest to fix. Yet Christians still need to take it seriously. Why? First, because when we allow one relationship to crowd out others, we lose perspective. In Proverbs 15:22 we read, "Plans fail for lack of counsel, but with many advisers they succeed." If we make our decisions about life based solely on the influence of one relationship, we'll probably make poor judgments.

Of course we make this same mistake in any number of non-romantic relationships. But we face this problem more often in dating relationships because these relationships involve our hearts and emotions. And because dating focuses on the plans of a couple, major issues related to marriage, family, and faith are likely at stake.

And if two people haven't defined their level of commitment, they're particularly at risk. You put yourself in a precarious position if you isolate yourself from the people who love and support you because you dive wholeheartedly into a romantic relationship not grounded in commitment. In *Passion and Purity,* Elisabeth Elliot states, "Unless a man is prepared to ask a woman to be his wife, what right has he to claim her exclusive attention? Unless she has been asked to marry him, why would a sensible woman promise any man her exclusive attention?" How many people end dating relationships only to find their ties to other friends severed?

When Garreth and Jenny mutually decided to stop dating, they were surprised to find their other friendships in disrepair. It's not that their other friends didn't like them; they hardly knew them anymore. Neither had invested any time or effort in maintaining these friendships while they concentrated on their dating relationship.

Perhaps you've done a similar thing. Or maybe you know the pain and frustration of being put on the back burner for the sake of a friend's boyfriend or girlfriend. The exclusive attention so often expected in dating relationships has a tendency to steal people's passion for serving in the church and to isolate them from the friends who love them most, family members who know them best, and, sadly, even God, whose will is far more important than any romantic interest.

5. Dating, in many cases, distracts young adults from their primary responsibility of preparing for the future.
We cannot live in the future, but neglecting our current obligations will disqualify us for tomorrow's responsibilities. Being distracted by love is not such a bad thing—unless God wants you to be doing something else.

One of the saddest tendencies of dating is to distract young adults from developing their God-given abilities and skills. Instead of equipping themselves with the character, education, and experience necessary to succeed in life, many allow themselves to be consumed by the present needs that dating emphasizes.

Christopher and Stephanie started dating when they were both fifteen years old. In many ways, they had the model dating relationship. They never got involved physically, and when they broke up two years later, their breakup was amicable. So what harm was done? Well, none in the sense that they didn't get into trouble. But we can begin to see some problems when we look at what Christopher and Stephanie could have been doing instead. Maintaining a relationship takes a lot of time and energy. Christopher and Stephanie spent countless hours talking, writing, thinking, and often worrying about their relationship. The energy they exerted stole from other pursuits. For

Christopher, the relationship drained his enthusiasm for his hobby of computer programming and his involvement with the church's worship band. Though Stephanie doesn't hold it against Christopher, she rejected several opportunities to go on short-term missions because she didn't want to be away from him. Their relationship swallowed up time both of them could have spent developing skills and exploring new opportunities.

Dating may help you practice being a good boyfriend or girlfriend, but what are these skills really worth? Even if you're going out with the person you will one day marry, a preoccupation with being the perfect boyfriend or girlfriend now can actually hinder you from being the future husband or wife that person will one day need.

6. *Dating can cause discontentment with God's gift of singleness.*
On my brother's third birthday, he received a beautiful blue bicycle. The miniature bike was brand-new, complete with training wheels, protective padding, and streamers. I thought he couldn't ask for a better first bike, and I couldn't wait to see his reaction.

But to my chagrin my brother didn't seem impressed with the present. When my dad pulled the bike out of its large cardboard box, my brother looked at it a moment, smiled, then began playing with the box. It took my family and me a few days to convince him that the real gift was the bike.

I can't help but think that God views our infatuation with short-term dating relationships much as I did my brother's love for a worthless box. A string of uncommitted dating relationships is not the gift! God gives us singleness—a season of our lives unmatched in its boundless opportunities for growth, learning, and service—and we view it as a chance to get bogged down in finding and keeping boyfriends and girlfriends. But we don't find the real beauty of singleness in pursuing romance with as many different people as we want. We find the real beauty in using our freedom to serve God with abandon.

Dating causes dissatisfaction because it encourages a wrong use of this freedom. God has placed a desire in most men and women for marriage. Although we don't sin when we look forward to marriage, we might be guilty of poor stewardship of our singleness when we allow a desire for something God obviously doesn't have for us *yet* to rob our ability to enjoy and appreciate what He *has* given us. Dating plays a role in fostering this dissatisfaction because it gives single people just enough intimacy to make them wish they had more. Instead of enjoying the unique qualities of singleness, dating causes people to focus on what they don't have.

7. *Dating creates an artificial environment for evaluating another person's character.*
Although most dating relationships don't head toward marriage, some—especially those among older, college-age students—are motivated by marriage. People who sincerely want to find out if someone is potential marriage material need to understand that typical dating actually hinders that process. Dating creates an artificial environment for two people to interact. As a result, each person can easily convey an equally artificial image.

In the driveway of our house we have a basketball hoop that we can adjust to different heights. When I lower the hoop three feet from its normal setting, I can look like a pretty good basketball player. Dunking is no problem. I glide across the pavement and slam the ball down every time. But my "skill" exists only because I've lowered the standards—I'm not playing in a real environment. Put me on a court with a ten-foot hoop, and

I'm back to being a white boy who can't jump.

In a similar way, dating creates an artificial environment that doesn't demand a person to accurately portray his or her positive and negative characteristics. On a date, a person can charm his or her way into a date's heart. He drives a nice car and pays for everything; she looks great. But who cares? Being fun on a date doesn't say anything about a person's character or ability to be a good husband or wife.

Part of the reason dating is fun is that it gives us a break from real life. For this reason, when I'm married I plan to make a habit of dating my wife. In marriage, you *need* to take breaks from the stress of kids and work; you need to just get away for a bit. But two people weighing the possibility of marriage need to make sure they don't just interact within the fun, romantic settings of dating. Their priority shouldn't be to get away from real life; they need a strong dose of objective reality! They need to see each other in the real-life settings of family and friends. They need to watch each other serving and working. How does he interact with the people who know him best? How does she react when things don't go perfectly? When considering a potential mate, we need to find the answers to these kinds of questions—questions that dating won't answer.

OLD HABITS DIE HARD

The seven habits of highly defective dating reveal that we can't fix many of dating's problems by merely "dating right." I believe that dating has dangerous tendencies that don't go away just because Christians do the steering. And even those Christians who can avoid the major pitfalls of premarital sex and traumatic breakups often spend much of their energy wrestling with temptation.

If you've dated, this probably sounds familiar to you. I think that for too long we've approached relationships using the world's mind-set and values, and if you've tried it, you might agree with me that it just doesn't work. Let's not waste any more time battling the swerving cart of dating. It's time for a new attitude.

CHAPTER THREE

A New Attitude

FIVE ATTITUDE CHANGES TO HELP YOU AVOID DEFECTIVE DATING

In the previous chapter, I outlined the seven habits of highly defective dating. Perhaps that chapter challenged the way you think about dating. If so, you're probably saying to yourself, "I can agree that dating has its problems. But what do I do now? *How* do Christians avoid defective dating?"

The first step is to change your attitude toward relationships. Easier said than done, right? But in Ephesians 4:22–24 (NLT), Paul shows us how we can transform our lives: "...throw off your old evil nature and your former way of life, which is rotten through and through, full of lust and deception. Instead, there must be a spiritual renewal of your thoughts and attitudes. You must display a new person because you are a new person, created in God's likeness—righteous, holy and true." Until we renew our way of thinking about love and relationships, our lifestyles will continue to flounder in the mire of defective dating.

In this chapter, I'd like to clearly state the perspective that I believe God wants us to have toward romance. What follows are five important "new attitudes" that will help us break out of dating's negative habits. Each of these flows from our view of three areas: love, purity, and singleness. We'll expand on these three areas in the next section, but for now the attitude changes described here give a glimpse of the practical alternative God offers those who want His best.

1. Every relationship is an opportunity to model Christ's love.

Bethany, an outgoing freshman at a Christian college, has a reputation as a bit of a flirt. Unfortunately, much of her interaction with guys is fake—it focuses on attracting attention to herself and getting a reaction from whoever she currently likes. Bethany invests more energy in getting a guy to like her than she does in spurring him toward godliness.

But when Bethany changes her perspective and realizes her friendships with guys are opportunities to love them as Christ does, she takes a 180 degree turn from flirtatiousness to honest, sincere love that treats guys as brothers, not potential boyfriends. Instead of viewing herself as the center of the universe with other people revolving around her, she can begin to look for ways to bless others.

The world will know we follow Christ by the way we love others. For this reason, we must practice love as God defines it—sincere, servant-hearted, and selfless—not the world's brand of selfish and sensual love based on what feels good.

2. My unmarried years are a gift from God.

Michael is twenty-one years old and has an engaging personality that matches his good looks. As the intern for his church's youth ministry, he has more than enough opportunities to meet and get to know Christian girls. Although he realizes his potential for ministry as a single and doesn't feel rushed to get married, he has developed a pattern of dating one girl after another. Although Michael has done nothing immoral, his pattern of short-term dating potentially robs him of the flexibility, freedom, and focus of singleness. He still operates from the old dating mind-set that he's incomplete without a girlfriend.

But when Michael adopts a new attitude that views singleness as a gift, he learns to be content with friendship during the time God wants him to remain single. As a result, Michael can clear his life of the clutter that short-term relationships contribute to his life. With this newly freed time and energy, Michael can pursue more effective ministry and deeper friendships with people of both genders.

Until you realize God's gift of your singleness, you'll probably miss out on the incredible opportunities it holds. Perhaps even now you can think of an opportunity you could grasp if you let go of the dating mind-set. As a single you have the freedom right now to explore, study, and tackle the world. No other time in your life will offer these chances.

3. *Intimacy is the reward of commitment—I don't need to pursue a romantic relationship before I'm ready for marriage.*
Jenny is seventeen and has dated a boy from her church for over a year. They're both strong Christians, and they want to marry each other someday. The "someday" part is the problem—realistically, they can't get married for quite a few years. Both have specific things to accomplish for God before they can take that step.

The old attitude would say that intimacy feels good, so enjoy it now. But the new attitude recognizes that if two people can't make a commitment to each other, they don't have any business pursuing romance. Even though it isn't easy, Jenny tells her boyfriend that they need to limit the time and energy they invest in each other. Trusting that God can bring them back together if He wills, they halt their progression of intimacy until they can match it with commitment. Though they struggle with the separation, missing the closeness they once enjoyed, they know in the long run—whether they marry each other or someone else—they've made the best choice for both of them.

God has made each of us with a desire for intimacy, and He intends to fulfill it. While we're single He doesn't expect these longings to disappear, but I believe He asks us to have the patience to wait and, in the meantime, seek close relationships with family and deep, non-romantic relationships with brothers and sisters in the Lord.

This doesn't mean you have to marry the first person with whom you find both romance and intimacy. While I do know some people who have married the first person with whom they developed an intimate, romantic relationship, most of us won't follow this path. Each of us will probably develop intimate relationships with several people before God clearly indicates who to marry. But we can't use this reality as an excuse to pursue romance for its own sake. I believe this mind-set is misguided and selfish. If you're not ready to consider marriage or you're not truly interested in marrying a specific person, why encourage that person to need you or ask him or her to meet your needs emotionally or physically?

4. I cannot "own" someone outside of marriage.
In God's eyes two married people become one. And as you continue to mature, you'll often crave the oneness that comes from sharing life with someone. Perhaps you feel that desire even now. Yet I believe that until we're ready to commit our lives in marriage, we have no right to treat anyone as if he or she belongs to us.

Sarah and Philip are both seniors in high school and have gone out with each other for six months. Their relationship has reached a fairly serious level. In fact, for all intents and purposes, they might as well be married. They rarely do anything apart—they monopolize each other's weekends, drive each other's cars, and know each other's families almost as well as their own. As well, their physical relationship is fairly serious. In fact, it's in a precarious position. Even though they haven't had sex, they constantly struggle with going too far.

The old attitude says we can "play marriage" if we really love someone. But the new attitude views a claim on another person's time, affection, and future before marriage as unwarranted.

Sarah and Philip realize they need to end their relationship as it now exists. By staking a claim on each other, they've stifled their individual growth and needlessly consumed energy that they should have directed into service and preparation for the future. They've planned their lives around each other when they don't really know that they'll get married someday. And in reality, if they are like most high school couples, each of them will probably marry someone else.

Even if Sarah and Philip had kept their physical relationship completely pure, they still would have made unwarranted claims on each other's spiritual and emotional life by continuing the relationship. If God wants them together in the future, their current decision to halt their involvement won't endanger His plan. Right now they need to obey God and break up a relationship that has them stealing from each other.

Are you making unwarranted emotional, spiritual, or even physical claims on someone? Ask God to show you whether you need to reevaluate a current relationship.

5. *I will avoid situations that could compromise the purity of my body or mind.*

Jessica, age sixteen, is a good girl who is unfortunately very naive. Even though she's a virgin and has committed to saving sex for marriage, she places herself in compromising situations with her older boyfriend—homework at her house when her mom's gone, hiking alone, ending their dates in his parked car. If Jessica were honest, she'd admit that she likes the excitement of these situations. She thinks it's very romantic, and it gives her a feeling of control over her boyfriend who, to be quite honest, will go as far in their physical relationship as Jessica will allow.

But when Jessica takes on a new attitude, she sees that purity consists of more than remaining a virgin. When she honestly examines her relationship with her boyfriend, she realizes that she has left the *direction* of purity. To get back on course she has to drastically change her lifestyle. First, she ends the relationship with her boyfriend because they focus on the physical aspect. Then she commits to fleeing those settings that lend themselves to compromise.

Where, when, and with whom you choose to spend your time reveals your true commitment to purity. Do you need to examine your tendencies? If you do, make sure that you avoid placing yourself in settings that encourage temptation.

UNNECESSARY BAGGAGE

Right now you might be thinking, "This new attitude is radical!" Maybe you're wondering whether you can adopt such seemingly foreign attitudes. I know that this new attitude challenges convention and even habits you may have already adopted. But I believed that if we want to live the "God-fashioned life" we must embrace a revolutionary pattern of living. In its wild abandonment to obedience, the God-fashioned life leaves no room for pettiness, insincerity, wasted time, or selfishness. In short, it is a lifestyle that leaves no room for the seven habits of highly defective dating.

This may sound too difficult to you. But if you give it some consideration, I think you might find it doable, even desirable. Why? Because the Christian with his or her eyes on the goal of sincere and intelligent love will find throwing out the world's approach to relationships as no sacrifice. Rejecting the old attitude is the natural response to not only the evident problems in dating, but more important, to the high calling we've received from God. He commands us to "throw off everything that hinders" and "run with perseverance the race marked out for us" (Hebrews 12:1). God wants us to win the race of life. The attitudes and practices of our culture's dating relationships are unnecessary baggage that weighs us down.

"But what's the alternative?" you ask. Loneliness? Lifelong singleness? Friday nights at home watching videos with your cat? No! No! No!

Choosing to quit the dating game doesn't mean rejecting friendship with the opposite sex, companionship, romance, or marriage. We still can pursue these things; we just choose to pursue them on God's terms and in His time. God asks us to put our romantic ambitions in the "all these things" pile that we must leave behind so we can "seek first his kingdom and his righteousness" (Matthew 6:33). Leaving dating behind is a side effect of God's primary desire for us to consume ourselves with seeking Him wholeheartedly.

MAKING THE TRADE

Many of the attitudes and practices of today's dating relationships conflict with the lifestyle of smart love God wants us to live. Let me ask you some tough, soul-searching questions. Are you willing to break our culture's rules to experience God's best? Are you willing to give Him everything, committing yourself to Him with abandon?

A simple story told by one of my favorite preachers, Ravi Zacharias, clearly illustrates the choice we face. One day a boy who has a bag of marbles proposes a trade with a little girl who has a bag of candy. The girl gladly agrees. But while the boy gets out his marbles, he realizes that he can't bear to part with some of them. Rather dishonestly, he takes three of his best marbles and hides them under his pillow. The boy and girl make the trade, and the girl never knows he has cheated her. But that night while the girl lies fast asleep, the boy has no peace. He's wide awake, pondering a question that nags him: "I wonder if she kept her best candy, too?"

Like that little boy, many of us walk through life plagued by the question "Has God given me His best?" But the question that we must answer first is "Am I giving God *my* best?"

You and I will never experience God's best—in singleness or in marriage—until we give God our all. We've held onto old attitudes, foolishly clutching a lifestyle that the world tells us will bring fulfillment. God asks us to hand them all over to Him.

Where are you right now? Have you given God everything within you, or do you still hold your favorite marbles in your hands, including your attitude about dating?

In the following chapters we'll examine our attitudes toward three heart issues—love, patience, and purity—that shape our approach to relationships. As we seek to gain God's perspective, we'll discover that giving Him everything is well worth the trade.

PART TWO

The Heart
of the Matter

CHAPTER FOUR

Looking Up "Love" in God's Dictionary

LEARNING THE TRUE DEFINITION OF LOVE

Y ou did what?" I asked in disbelief.

Jeff laughed loudly and accelerated the car as we went around a turn. My shock apparently energized him. "Gloria told her mom she was staying at her friend's house, and we rented a room at a hotel Friday night," he said as if it were no big deal.

Though he hardly seemed old enough to be driving, my sixteen-year-old friend was acting as my chauffer during the summer weeks I spent at my grandmother's home in Ohio. Our parents had known each other since the couples were newly-weds; we had pictures playing together as preschoolers.

Jeff and his girlfriend, Gloria, had been going out for a while. If you didn't count the numerous times they had broken up then reconciled, they had dated for almost a year. Jeff had always remained vague about their level of physical involvement, but now they had obviously fully consummated their relationship.

"We got a room at the Holiday Inn in Dayton," he explained as he put his hand out the window into the cool night air. Turning to me he grinned, winked mischievously, and said, "Man, oh, man."

"I can't believe you," I said, letting the tone of my voice convey my disapproval. "You mean you and Gloria had...you had...I mean you slept together?"

Jeff could tell I wasn't pleased. He wanted me to be impressed, to slap him on the back like one of his football teammates in the locker room and praise him for his "exploit." I wanted to slap him all right, but not on the back.

"Look, Josh," he said defensively, "we've waited a long time for this. It was really special. Maybe it doesn't meet your morals, but we felt that it was the right time to show our love."

"My morals?" I said indignantly. "My morals? Since when were they mine? How many times have we talked about this? With each other? At church? Jeff, you know that wasn't right. You..."

"We love each other," Jeff said, cutting me off in midsentence. "If you ever really fall in love, then you'll understand."

The conversation ended. For some reason the stoplight took forever to turn green. We sat silently as the turn signal clicked off and on. I looked out the window.

Four years later, Jeff was going to college in Michigan. "I'm engaged!" he told me over the phone. "Debbie is incredible. I've never been so in love."

"That's great," I said. My congratulations sounded hollow. I couldn't help it. I was thinking of Gloria. I hadn't seen her for a long time. What was she now? Three or four girlfriends back? Love, huh?

THE FIRST KISS

"How does Chinese sound?" I asked as we pulled out of the driveway.

"Hey, that's great," Eric replied with his typical enthusiasm.

I'd only just met Eric and his wife, Leslie, but had already noted Eric's exuberance and excitement about everything—even my restaurant suggestion.

"That all right with you, honey?" he gently asked Leslie, who was sitting in the back seat.

"Sure," she replied sweetly.

Eric and Leslie had stopped by to visit me during a drive through the Northwest. A friend in Colorado had told me about these newlyweds and the little book they had written. Their book told the story of how they had met and grown to love each other without following the typical pattern of dating.

You'd be hard pressed to find two more romantic people. They adored each other, and it showed. Eric rarely took his eyes off Leslie. Sitting in the passenger seat on the way to the restaurant, he slipped his hand behind the seat, and Leslie reached forward and clasped it. Holding hands when one person is sitting in the front seat and the other is in the back? I'd never seen that before.

After dinner, while we cracked open our fortune cookies, I had a question. "You two can't keep your hands off each other," I began teasingly. Leslie blushed. "Was it difficult keeping the physical side of your relationship pure while you were engaged?"

Eric took Leslie's hand and smiled at her before he answered. "Of course the desire for that was present—it always will be," he said. "But no, it wasn't a struggle. Leslie and I decided very early in our relationship that we were going to refrain from physical contact until we were married. Our first kiss was at the altar."

My jaw dropped. "You didn't kiss until you got married?"

"Nope," Eric said, beaming. "The most we did was hold hands. And, Josh, we know that kind of standard isn't for every couple. We didn't make that decision to be legalistic; it came from the heart. Everyone, even our parents, told us we should kiss. But we both decided it was what we wanted to do. It was a way to show our love, to protect each other before we were married." And then with a twinkle in his eye, he said, "Let me tell you, Josh, that first kiss was the most incredible, beautiful thing in the world. I can't even begin to describe it."

Eric and Leslie. Jeff and Gloria. Two couples that used the same word—love—to explain what motivated them to act in opposite ways. Were both couples talking about the same thing? For Jeff and Gloria, love justified a night in a hotel room enjoying each other's bodies before marriage. For Eric and Leslie, love meant barely touching each other before they walked to the altar. For Jeff and Gloria, love was impatient and demanded compromise. For Eric and Leslie, love fueled integrity and gave them the patience needed to wait.

One word. Two definitions.

IN LOVE WITH LOVE

I am, by my own admission, a hopeless romantic. If such a thing is possible, I am in love with being in love.

There's nothing else quite like it, and if you've experienced it, you know what I mean. Being in love is a patchwork of a thousand indescribable moments. Nervous energy runs through your body whenever you think of that special person, which is every waking minute. You lose interest in the dull chores of eating, sleeping, and thinking rationally. You discover that every love song on the radio was written for you. It seems that someone has removed blinders from your eyes, and you can see the world full of wonder and mystery and happiness.

I love love. But I've come to realize that I don't really know much about it. Oh, I can tell you all about the warm, fuzzy side of love. I can throw myself into romance with all the passion of Romeo, but in God's school of true love, I'm afraid I'm still in kindergarten.

To me and other romantics who share a "love for love," God wants to give a higher, grander view. He wants to deepen our understanding. Romance can thrill us to our core, but it's only a small part of true love. We've been playing in the sandbox—God wants to take us to the beach.

APHRODITE OR CHRIST?

I cannot overemphasize the importance of gaining God's perspective on love. We can link all of the negative habits of dating to adopting a fallen world's attitudes toward love. And the conflict between God's definition of love and the world's is not new. Christians have always had a choice to either imitate the Master or slip into the more enticing pattern for love provided by the world.

The apostle Paul understood this struggle when he wrote his famous chapter on love to the Christians living in Corinth. He must have realized the irony of his task. In Paul's day, writing to Corinthians about God's love was the equivalent of writing a letter on family values to Hollywood today. "Corinthian" was synonymous with immorality. To "play the Corinthian" meant to give oneself to sexual pleasure. A "Corinthian girl" was another word for a prostitute. How could Paul hope to convey an understanding of God's pure love to a city steeped in perversion?

Love is patient, love is kind. It does not envy, it does not boast, it is not proud (1 Corinthians 13:4).

The bustling, cosmopolitan, port town had elevated sex to a religious pursuit. The temple of Aphrodite, the Greek goddess of love, employed one thousand prostitutes. How could these people possibly understand the true meaning of the statement "God is love" (1 John 4:16) when on every street corner and from every brothel someone offered their version of "love"—sensual pleasure—to them? Would they see the truth and beauty of real love in the midst of the seductiveness of its counterfeit?

It is not rude, it is not self-seeking, it is not easily angered, it keeps no record of wrongs (1 Corinthians 13:5).

Would Aphrodite or Christ triumph in Corinth? Would sensuality push out servanthood? Would sexuality have priority over selflessness? Would the readers of Paul's humble letter choose the everlasting or the fleeting pleasure of the moment?

Today Christians endure the very same struggle. Though separated by some two thousand years, similarities abound between our culture and that of Corinth. More than ever, sex is a commodity. Sensuality and exaggerated sexuality shout at us on every corner, if not from brothels then from newsstands and billboards. "Love is sex," a Calvin Klein ad whispers. "Sex is pleasure," a movie tells us. And on the radio, "Pleasure is all that matters" is sung sweetly in our ears.

In the midst of this harangue, God's quiet message of true love still speaks to those who choose to listen.

Can you hear it? Put down the magazine. Turn off the VCR. Pull the plug on the stereo and listen...

Love does not delight in evil but rejoices with the truth. It always protects, always trusts, always hopes, always perseveres.
Love never fails (1 Corinthians 13: 6–8).

FASHION NIGHTMARE

Like the Christians in Corinth, we have two styles of love to select from—God's or the world's. Which will we choose?

I have an image that may help us understand our role as followers of Christ and therefore the style of love we should adopt. You may think it sounds strange at first, but stick with me. It will make sense as I explain. I think we should view love as something we wear.

From the day Adam and Eve disobeyed God then donned fig leaves in the Garden of Eden, the world has experienced something of a fashion nightmare, not in terms of clothing but in terms of love. When sin marred God's original design for love, the human race began "wearing" a twisted, corrupted imitation based on selfishness and irresponsibility.

But because God's love is perfect and enduring, He created a way for us to experience His design for love once again. He sent Jesus Christ to set things straight. In fashion terms, we could call the Author and Finisher of our faith the Designer and Model of a revolutionary expression of love. Christ gave His life for a world that rejected Him, and he told us to love our enemies. He washed the feet of the men who called him Master and told us to serve each other in humility.

He gave us the pattern— "As I have loved you, so you must love one another" (John 13:34)—and told us to share it with the world.

SUPER MODELS

You may never model high fashion in New York or Paris, but as a Christian you model God's love to the world. Understanding this role profoundly affects our approach to relationships, especially our dating relationships. When dating we represent God's love, not only to the other person in the relationship, but also to the people watching us.

As Christians, we need to remember that God's perfect love is not only for our benefit. A model wears clothing to attract attention to the designer's creativity. The model displays the designer's work, but the designer's reputation is on the line, not the model's. In the same way, as Christians we model God's love, whether or not we realize it. People watch us, and what they see affects God's reputation for loving His creation. If we claim to follow Christ then wear the world's twisted style of love, we drag the name and character of our Lord in the dirt.

For this reason, we must ask ourselves, "Am I modeling the love of Christ? Do my motivations and actions in this relationship reflect the perfect love God has shown me?" How would you answer those questions right now?

I LOVE ME

I believe that we can model God's perfect love when we avoid the negative habits of dating. And doing this requires recognizing and rejecting the world's pattern of love. First we must understand that all of the world's deceptions flow from the belief that *love is primarily for the fulfillment and comfort of self.* The world poisons love by focusing on meeting one's own needs first and foremost.

We witness this poison in the boyfriend or girlfriend who pressures a partner into sex. You've heard the line "If you really loved me you'd do it." In other words, "I don't care about you, your convictions, or how this could damage you emotionally— meet *my* needs!" Or what about the person who dates someone because it will boost his or her own popularity but then dumps that person when someone in a higher social stratum comes along? While the first example is more extreme, both examples illustrate self-centered "love" in action.

Next we're told that *love is primarily a feeling.* At first glance this seems innocent enough—we often feel love, and this isn't necessarily wrong. But when we make feelings the litmus test of love, we place *ourselves* at the center of importance. By themselves, our feelings don't do others one bit of good. If a man "feels" love for the poor but never gives money to help them or never shows kindness to them, what are his feelings worth? They may benefit him, but if his actions don't communicate this love, his feelings mean nothing.

By inflating the importance of feelings, we neglect the importance of putting love into action. When we evaluate the quality of our love for someone else simply by our own emotional fulfillment, we practice selfishness.

I'VE FALLEN AND I CAN'T GET UP

The second common fallacy about love deals with personal responsibility. The world tells us that *love is beyond our control.*

This thinking has found its way into our language. We describe the beginning of a passionate relationship as "falling in love." Or people say, "We're madly in love with each other." You've more than likely heard people say these things—perhaps you've even said them yourself.

Why do we feel compelled to compare love to a pit or a mental disorder? What do these statements reveal about our attitudes toward love? I think we make these somewhat overstated analogies because they remove personal responsibility. If a person falls into a pit, what can she do about it? If an animal contracts rabies and runs around foaming at the mouth and biting people, it can't really help its nasty behavior because it has gone mad.

Does it sound a little absurd to discuss love in such terms? I think so. Yet we tend to express our experience of love in these ways. We think of love as something beyond our control and thus excuse ourselves from having to behave responsibly. In extreme cases, people have blamed love for immorality, murder, rape, and many other sins. Okay, so maybe you and I haven't done those things. But perhaps you've lied to parents or friends because of a relationship. Maybe you pushed your partner too far physically. But if love is out of our control, we can't possibly be held responsible. Yes, we know we behaved rashly. Yes, we know we might have hurt others in the process, but we couldn't help it. We were in love.

A SLAP IN THE FACE

The world may define and defend love in these terms, but the Bible offers a very different perspective. For the person practicing the self-centered, feeling-governed, beyond-my-control love of the world, God's definition can be as startling as an unexpected slap in the face.

The world takes us to a silver screen on which flickering images of passion and romance play, and as we watch, the world says, "This is love." God takes us to the foot of a tree on which a naked and bloodied man hangs and says, "*This* is love."

God always defines love by pointing to His Son. The Word became flesh and dwelt among us to give a point of reference, a living, breathing, revolutionary example of true love. And Christ's antidote to the poison of self-love is the cross. "If anyone would come after me," Jesus said, "he must deny himself and take up his cross and follow me" (Matthew 16:24).

Christ taught that *love is not for the fulfillment of self but for the good of others and the glory of God.* True love is selfless. It gives; it sacrifices; it dies to its own needs. "Greater love has no one than this," Jesus said, "that he lay down his life for his friends" (John 15:13). He backed up His words with His actions—He laid down His life first for all of us.

Christ also showed that *true love is not measured or governed by feeling.* He went to the cross when every emotion and instinct in his body told him to turn back. Have you ever read the account of Jesus' praying in the Garden of Gethsemane? He clearly didn't *feel* like enduring the beatings, hanging on the cross, and giving up His life. But He laid His feelings before the Father, giving Himself over to the Father's will. Jesus' feelings were not the test of His love, nor were they His master.

Christ wants us to have this same attitude. He did not say, "If you love me, you will feel warm, cascading sensations of religious emotion." Instead he told us, "If you love me, you will obey what I command" (John 14:15). True love always expresses itself in obedience to God and service to others. Good feelings are nice but not necessary.

Jesus' example also shows us that *love is under our control.* He *chose* to love us. He chose to lay down his life for us. The danger of believing that you "fall in love" is that it also means you can "fall out of love" just as unexpectedly. Aren't you glad that God's love for us isn't as unpredictable? Aren't you thankful that God's love is under His control and not based on whim? We need to throw out the misconception that love is some strange "force" that tosses us around like leaves in the wind against our will. We cannot justify doing what we know is wrong by saying that "love" grabbed hold of us and "made" us behave irresponsibly. That's not love. Instead, it's what the Bible calls in 1 Thessalonians 4:5 "passionate lust." We express true love in obedience to God and service to others—not reckless or selfish behavior—and we *choose* these behaviors.

TRUE LOVE NULLIFIES DATING

With these truths about love in place, let's make a practical application. If dating hinges on our attitude toward love, what happens to dating when we take on Christ's attitudes?

Sparks fly.

God's true love pretty much nullifies dating as we know it. Think about it—when you date guided by the world's attitude that love is for the benefit of self, you base your dating decisions on what's best for you. I opened this chapter with a story about my friends Jeff and Gloria. Unfortunately, they often subscribed to the world's definition of love. First, their motivation was self-centered. Jeff went out with Gloria because she was pretty, other guys liked her, and she satisfied him sexually. His criteria for pursuing a relationship with her compares to his criteria for choosing a pair of jeans—makes me feel good, makes me look good. Gloria wasn't much better. She liked Jeff because he was a "prize"—he was good-looking and athletic, and he owned a nice car. They met each other's emotional and physical needs and helped each other's image.

But had they turned away from the world's self-centered attitude, many of the "good reasons" for pursuing romance in dating would have begun to disappear. What if Jeff and Gloria had asked, "What is my *real* reason for seeing this person romantically? What am I seeking that couldn't be found in a friendship? Am I selfishly seeking only my own fulfillment? What am I communicating to him (or her)? Am I arousing emotions I'm not ready to meet? Will he (or she) be hurt if I allow this relationship to proceed now? Is this relationship going to help or hinder his (or her) walk with God?" We need to start asking ourselves these kinds of questions. Is this other-focused attitude more complicated? Maybe. More godly? Definitely. Our entire motivation is transformed when we extract the poison of self-love.

More changes occur when we seek to love with Christ's love. Jeff and Gloria bought into the world's assumption that love was beyond their control. Their feelings governed their actions. They were enslaved to what 1 John 2:16 calls the "cravings of sinful man" and "the lust of his eyes." They often used "being in love" as an excuse for disobeying God. In their physical relationship, they grabbed at all they could within—and ultimately outside—the boundaries set before marriage. They ended up lying to their parents and violating each other's purity, all in the name of love. Feelings governed them, and finally, when the feelings ended, so did their relationship.

But what if Jeff and Gloria had realized that they would answer to God for their actions—regardless of whether or not they were "in love"? They would have told their feelings to take a hike.

The same is true for you and me. We need to forget our sinful instincts! By nature, our instincts want to set us on a course of destruction. We shouldn't allow our feelings to set the tone or the pace for our relationships. Instead, we need to allow wisdom and patience and selflessness to guide us.

"LOVE MUST BE SINCERE"

As we seek to love according to God's design, we must pursue sincerity. "Love must be sincere"—this brief command given in Romans 12:9 leaves no room for misunderstanding. The love God wants His children to live by has no room for deceit and hypocrisy—it has to be genuine and earnest.

Unfortunately, much of what takes place between guys and girls today is insincere. There is nearly always an angle, a hidden agenda. What can you do for me? What can I get from you?

I'll never forget a conversation I sat through with a group of guys. Girls, you would have been appalled if you had overheard it. These guys were discussing things a guy could do on a date to get a girl to fall for him. They recited lines for stirring the heart and lines for getting a kiss. One guy explained his technique of alternating warmth with disinterest and coolness—he claimed that this approach kept a girl guessing and trying her best to please him. Another guy shared ways to put a girl in a romantic mood. He'd take a date to a furniture store, and as he and the girl walked through the displays, he would talk about families and ask which tables and couches she would want for her home someday. "Girls go nuts for this!" he told us. He explained that with marriage and future plans on her mind, the girl would more likely be romantic and affectionate during the evening.

Bluntly put, this conversation was a study in manipulation. All of it was completely fake, completely insincere. The guys didn't seek ways to bless girls. They merely wanted ways to push emotional buttons to get something for themselves.

I'm sure many girls would admit to having their own set of tricks. But no matter how commonplace or ingrained in our culture these practices may be, we all face judgment by the four simple words given by God: "Love must be sincere."

We need to embrace the incredible responsibility we bear as representatives of Christ's love here on earth. "By this all men will know that you are my disciples," Jesus said, "if you love one another" (John 13:35). The world will know we are different, the world will see a glimpse of the divine, saving love of God by the way we love. Will others see the sincerity of Christ's love in our relationships? Or will they see the same brand of self-centered love practiced by the world and turn away in disappointment?

Practice Makes Perfect—or Perfectly Imperfect

The love we practice in dating not only shows the world Christ's love, it also prepares us for our future relationships. As we relate to others today, we form patterns that we'll take with us into our marriages. For this reason, we must not only practice sincere love but also practice commitment-based love.

We see so much divorce and betrayal in our society today. Take a quick count—how many of your friends come from broken homes? I believe that this trend will only increase as each generation begins to practice short-term love in dating relationships earlier and earlier. It seems that dating as we have come to know it doesn't really prepare us for marriage; instead it can be a training ground for divorce. We cannot practice life-long commitment in a series of short-term relationships.

Does that mean we're supposed to marry the first person we date? No. We need to carefully and cautiously consider marriage, remaining willing to back out of a relationship if God shows us we need to. There's no wisdom in rushing into marriage simply because we've become romantically attached to someone. The wrong mind-set so prevalent today, however, is not related to choosing a spouse. Many of us have fallen prey to the idea that we can, and should, pursue romance for its own sake. In other words, "I'll become intimate with you because it feels good, not because I'm prayerfully considering marriage." This attitude is not fair to the other person and is terrible preparation for marriage. Who wants to marry someone who will ditch a relationship the moment romantic feelings wane? Who wants to marry a person who has developed a habit of breaking up and finding someone new when the going gets tough?

We need to realize that the lifelong commitment so many of us desire in our future marriages cannot be practiced or prepared for in a lifestyle of short-term relationships. Until we can commit to making a relationship work for the rest of our lives—and yes, it is a huge commitment—we do ourselves and others a disservice by pursuing short-term love in the meantime. True love waits, but not just for sex. It waits for the right time to commit to God's brand of love—unwavering, unflagging, and totally committed.

PUSHING OUT PETTINESS

Committed, sincere, selfless, responsible—all these words describe God's love. And each stands in stark contrast to the love practiced by the world.

Our brief examination leads us to one simple conclusion: We cannot love as God loves and date as the world dates. God's grand view of love pushes out the pettiness and selfishness which defines so much of what takes place in dating.

Maybe some ideas in this chapter have sparked your interest, and you're wondering, "How should I respond?" I have some ideas. You may find them challenging; perhaps you'll disagree. But I must clearly state my convictions here. In my view, if dating encourages us to wear the world's style of love, then dating needs to go. If dating causes us to practice selfish, feeling-governed love that's contrary to God's love, we must kiss dating goodbye. We must stop trying to fit God's ideas into the lifestyles society has defined for us and allow His values and attitudes to redefine the way we live.

CHAPTER FIVE

The Right Thing at the Wrong Time Is the Wrong Thing

HOW TO KEEP IMPATIENCE FROM ROBBING YOU
OF THE GIFT OF SINGLENESS

I n *The Book of Virtues,* William J. Bennett tells a story called "The Magic Thread." In this French tale we read of Peter, a boy who is strong and able yet sadly flawed by an attitude of impatience. Always dissatisfied with his present condition, Peter spends his life daydreaming about the future.

One day while wandering in the forest, Peter meets a strange, old woman who gives him a most tantalizing opportunity—the chance to skip the dull, mundane moments of life. She hands Peter a silver ball from which a tiny, gold thread protrudes. "This is your life thread," she explains. "Do not touch it and time will pass normally. But if you wish time to pass more quickly, you have only to pull the thread a little way and an hour will pass like a second. But I warn you, once the thread has been pulled out, it cannot be pushed back in again."

This magical thread seems the answer to all of Peter's problems. It is just what he has always wanted. He takes the ball and runs home.

The following day in school Peter has his first opportunity to put the silver ball to use. The lesson is dragging, and the teacher scolds Peter for not concentrating. Peter fingers the silver ball and gives the thread a slight tug. Suddenly the teacher dismisses the class, and Peter is free to leave school. He is overjoyed! How easy his life will now be. From this moment, Peter begins to pull the thread a little every day.

But soon Peter begins to use the magic thread to rush through larger portions of life. Why waste time pulling the thread just a little every day when he can pull it hard and complete school altogether? He does so and finds himself out of school and apprenticed in a trade. Peter uses the same technique to rush through his engagement to his sweetheart. He cannot bear to wait months to marry her, so he uses the gold thread to hasten the arrival of his wedding day.

Peter continues this pattern throughout his life. When hard, trying times come, he escapes them with his magic thread. When the baby cries at night, when he faces financial struggles, when he wishes his own children to be launched in careers of their own, Peter pulls the magic thread and bypasses the discomfort of the moment.

But sadly, when he comes to the end of his life, Peter realizes the emptiness of such an existence. By allowing impatience and discontentment to rule him, Peter has robbed himself of life's richest moments and memories. With only the grave to look forward to, he deeply regrets ever having used the magic thread.

In introducing this story, Mr. Bennett insightfully comments, "Too often, people want what they want (or what they *think* they want, which is usually "happiness" in one form or another) *right now*. The irony of their impatience is that only by learning to wait, and by a willingness to accept the bad with the good, do we usually attain those things that are truly worthwhile."

DOES IMPATIENCE DICTATE OUR DATING?

I think we can gain valuable insight from Mr. Bennett's words as we examine the attitudes that guide dating. As we apply his words to the subject of this book, we move from the ethereal topic of love to the more concrete subject of timing. *When* we pursue romance is a major factor in determining whether or not dating is appropriate for us. And we can only determine the appropriate time to pursue romance when we understand God's purpose for singleness and trust *His* timing for relationships.

Dating as we now know it is often fueled by impatience, and we can directly relate many problems with dating to wrong timing. We want what we want right now. Though we don't possess a magical gold thread to rush us through life, we can develop wrong attitudes that have a similar effect. But God wants us to appreciate the gifts of the present season of our lives. He wants us to learn the patience and trust necessary to wait for his perfect timing in all things, including our love lives.

Let's examine three simple truths that can help adjust wrong attitudes toward the timing of relationships.

1. *The right thing at the wrong time is the wrong thing.*
As Americans, we don't readily accept the concept of delayed gratification. Our culture teaches us that if something is good we should seek to enjoy it immediately. So we microwave our food, e-mail our letters, and express mail our packages. We do our best to escape the confines of time by accelerating our schedules, speeding up our pace, and doing whatever it takes to beat the clock. You probably know exactly what I mean. How did you respond the last time you had to wait in line for something? Did you patiently wait your turn, or did you tap your toe and try to rush the experience?

Our "do it all now" mentality has tremendously affected the timing of today's dating relationships. Kids involve themselves in dating and even sexual relationships at an increasingly young age. As young people rush prematurely into these adult activities, most of their elders do little to correct them. After all, what can adults say when they live by the same "grab it all now" attitude?

Why do we insist on living this way? In my opinion, we adopt the immediate gratification mentality because we've lost sight of the biblical principle of seasons (see Ecclesiastes 3:1–8). Just as spring's role is different from that of fall, so each of the seasons of our lives has a different emphasis, focus, and beauty. One is not better than another; each season yields its own unique treasures. We cannot skip ahead to experience the riches of another life season any more than a farmer can rush the spring. Each season builds on the one before it.

God has many wonderful experiences He wants to give to us, but He also assigns these experiences to particular seasons of our lives. In our humanness, we often make the mistake of taking a good thing *out* of its appropriate season to enjoy it when *we* want it. Premarital sex is a prime example of this principle. Sex in itself is a wonderful experience (from what my married friends tell me), but if we indulge in it outside of God's plan, we sin. Like a fruit picked green or a flower plucked before it blossoms, our attempts to rush God's timing can spoil the beauty of His plan for our lives.

Just because something is good doesn't mean we should pursue it right now. We have to remember that the right thing at the wrong time is the wrong thing.

2. *You don't need to shop for what you can't afford.*
The timing of many dating relationships is equivalent to going shopping for an outfit when you don't have any money; even if

you find the "perfect fit," what can you do about it?

In chapter 3, the third "new attitude" addressed the importance of waiting for God's timing. It stated, "Intimacy is the reward of commitment—I don't need to pursue a romantic relationship before I'm ready for marriage."

We could restate this by saying, "Intimacy 'costs' commitment. If I'm not in a position to pay in the cold, hard 'cash' of commitment, I have no business 'going shopping' for my future mate."

Before two people are ready for the responsibility of commitment, they should content themselves with friendship and wait for romance and intimacy. Exercising this patience will not handicap them relationally. In friendship, they can practice the skills of relating, caring, and sharing their lives with other people. In friendship, they can observe other people's characters and begin to see what they'll one day want in their mates. While we can learn worthwhile lessons from dating relationships, we need to make sure these relationships don't bog us down. Wasting too much time trying each other out as boyfriend and girlfriend can actually distract two people from the more important task of preparing to be good spouses.

God has a perfect plan for your life. More than likely, that plan includes marriage, and if so, somewhere in this world God has the perfect person for you. You may or may not know this person right now. If you spend all your time and energy trying to hunt this person down or (if you've already found this person) trying to contain him or her until you can marry, you might actually do that person a disservice. The guy or girl you will one day marry doesn't need a girlfriend or boyfriend (even though he or she may want one right now). What that person really needs is someone mature enough to spend the season before marriage preparing to be a godly wife or husband.

Let's do our future spouses a favor and stop shopping around prematurely.

3. Any season of singleness is a gift from God.

Most of us won't remain single for our entire lives, and I think that we should view our singleness as a season of our lives, a gift from God. God gives an outline for the proper attitude toward singleness in 1 Corinthians 7:32. *The Message* translation reads:

> I want you to live as free of complications as possible. When you're unmarried, you're free to concentrate on simply pleasing the Master. Marriage involves you in all the nuts and bolts of domestic life and in wanting to please your spouse, leading to so many more demands on your attention. The time and energy that married people spend on caring for and nurturing each other, the unmarried can spend in becoming whole and holy instruments of God.

Paul doesn't say this to put marriage down. He says it to encourage us to view singleness as a gift. God doesn't use our singleness to punish us. He has created this season as an unparalleled opportunity for growth and service that we shouldn't take for granted or allow to slip by.

One person rightly stated, "Don't do something about your singlehood—do something *with* it!" Stop for just a minute and evaluate whether you're using God's gift of singleness as He desires. Ask yourself these questions: "Am I concentrating on 'simply pleasing the Master'? Am I using this season of my life to become a 'whole and holy' instrument for God? Or am I scrambling to find a romantic relationship with someone by dating? Could I possibly be throwing away the gift of single-ness? Am I cluttering my life with needless complications and worries of dating?"

While we're single, dating not only keeps us from preparing for marriage, it can quite possibly rob us of the gift of single-ness. Dating can tie us down in a series of pseudo relationships, but God wants us to maximize our freedom and flexibility to serve Him. Any season of singleness, whether you're sixteen or twenty-six, is a gift. You just might do God a disservice by wasting its potential on a lifestyle of short-term dating.

DO YOU REALLY TRUST HIM?

Though simply stated, these three truths bring about radical lifestyle changes when we apply them to our lives. To do so requires us to wait. That's right; God just asks us to wait. While you might not find that idea bold or daring or very impressive, it is obedient, and our obedience impresses God.

Waiting for God's timing requires trusting in God's good-ness. We develop patience as we trust that God denies us good things in the present only because He has something better for us in the future.

I'll freely admit it—I often have difficulty trusting God. When it comes to my love life, I have a nagging fear that He wants to keep me single forever. Or I fear that if He lets me marry, He'll match me up with some girl to whom I won't feel attracted.

I know these worries are silly. In my better moments I admit I haven't based these fears on the reality of the loving, caring Father in heaven whom I've come to know. But even though I know He's a good God, I often allow my lack of faith to affect the way I approach dating.

I fear God might forget me. Instead of trusting in His perfect timing, I often try to take things into my own hands. I grab my life's calendar from God and frantically begin to pencil in my own plans and agendas. "God, I know you're omnipotent and all that," I say, "but I really think you missed the fact that this girl over here is my destiny. If I don't go after her now, my future will pass me by!" Eventually I sheepishly hand back the scheduling of my time, energy, and attention, saying, "Of course I trust you, Lord, but I just think You could use a little help."

DATING AND MARSHMALLOWS

An article in *Time* magazine left this indelible image in my mind: a little child sitting alone in a room, staring at a marshmallow. This strange picture captures the feelings I sometimes have in my struggle to trust God to take care of my future marital status.

The article's subject was unrelated to dating—and marshmallows, too, for that matter. It was about actual research done with children. The first few paragraphs went this way:

It turns out that a scientist can see the future by watching four-year-olds interact with a marshmallow. The researcher invites the children, one by one, into a plain room and begins the gentle torment. "You can have this marshmallow right now," he says. "But if you wait while I run an errand, you can have two marshmallows when I get back." And then he leaves.

Some children grab the treat the minute he's out the door. Some last a few minutes before they give in. But others are determined to wait. They cover their eyes;

they put their heads down; they sing to themselves; they try to play games or even fall asleep. When the researcher returns, he gives these children their hard-earned marshmallows. And then, science waits for them to grow up.

By the time the children reach high school, something remarkable has happened. A survey of the children's parents and teachers found that those who as four-year-olds had the fortitude to hold out for the second marshmallow generally grew up to be better adjusted, more popular, adventurous, confident and dependable teenagers. The children who gave in to temptation early on were more likely to be lonely, easily frustrated and stubborn. They buckled under stress and shied away from challenges.

Of course, the moral of the story is that developing the character necessary to delay gratification in small areas can translate into great success in other areas. But the four-year-olds in the study didn't know that. They didn't resist the marshmallow in hopes of getting better grades in high school. They overcame their urge to eat the marshmallow because they had faith—they could envision the moment when the nice man in the white coat would come back with *two* marshmallows. They persevered because they trusted.

This story really encourages me. Sometimes as I wait on God's timing for romance, I go through the same internal struggle those kids must have endured. Like a marshmallow beckoning the child to eat its sweet fluffiness, dating is calling my name. And let me tell you, it looks *good*.

Why don't I snatch it up? Why shouldn't you? Because God has promised something better. He provides something better

now as we take advantage of the unique opportunities of singleness, and He'll provide something better *later* when we enter
into marriage. But we must have faith to believe it. Like those
little children, we're left alone with something that could possibly
satisfy us immediately. And we can't see the reward of delaying
our gratification.

It gets down to this question: Do you trust God? Don't just
give a knee-jerk, Sunday school answer. Do you *really* trust Him?
Do you live your life as if you trust Him? Do you believe that by
passing up something good now because it's the *wrong time* God
will bring you something better when it is the *right time?*

Jim and Elisabeth Elliot faced this difficult question in their
passionate relationship. They loved each other deeply, yet they
placed God's will before their own desires. In *Passion and Purity,*
Mrs. Elliot writes:

> We were being asked to trust to leave the planning to
> God. God's ultimate plan was as far beyond our imagin-
> ings as the oak tree is from the acorn's imaginings. The
> acorn does what it was made to do, without pestering its
> Maker with questions about when and how and why.
> We who have been given an intelligence and a will and a
> whole range of wants that can be set against the divine
> Pattern for Good are asked to believe Him. We are given
> the chance to trust Him when He says to us, '...If any
> man will let himself be lost for my sake, he will find his
> true self.'

> *When will we find it?* we ask. The answer is, *Trust Me.*
> *How will we find it?* The answer again is, *Trust Me.*
> *Why must I let myself be lost?* we persist. The answer is, *Look
> at the acorn and trust Me.*

GOD KNEW BEST

Many people realize too late that we don't arrive at contentment as a destination as much as we develop contentment as a state of mind. Paul tells us in 1 Timothy 6:6 that "godliness with contentment is great gain." And in Philippians 4:11 he writes, "I have learned to be content whatever the circumstances." What is Paul's secret?

Paul shares it with us: "I can do everything through him who gives me strength" (Philippians 4:13). Paul trusted God to give him strength to endure *any* situation he faced. In the same way, we can gain contentment when we trust in God's strength and God's grace to sustain us through any circumstance. Whether you're single or married; whether you're liked, loved, or lonely; the key to contentment is trust. Believe it or not, if we are discontented with singleness, we'll more than likely face discontentment when we're married. When we define our happiness by some point in the future, it will never arrive. We'll keep waiting until tomorrow. If we allow impatience to govern us, we will miss the gift of the moment. We'll arrive at that point in time that we expected to provide fulfillment and find it lacking.

One lady wrote to me, frustrated that people often view a single woman as just marking time until the right man comes along. "Poor single woman!" she continued. "The world wants her to fornicate, and the church wants her to marry! Whatever happened to what Paul said about the blessings of being single? William Booth, the founder of the Salvation Army, wrote, 'Don't instill, or allow anybody else to instill into the hearts of your girls the idea that marriage is the chief end of life. If you do, don't be surprised if they get engaged to the first empty, useless fool they come across.' Women (and men) should marry when it is plainly the will of God for their lives, not because they 'can't minister' otherwise, or because of social pressure." I can only add a hearty "Amen!" to her comments.

Author John Fischer, speaking as a single, young adult said, "God has called me to live now, not four years from now. He wants me to realize my full potential as a man right now, to be thankful for that, and to enjoy it to the fullest. I have a feeling that a single person who is always wishing he were married will probably get married, discover all that is involved, and wish he were single again. He will ask himself, 'Why didn't I use that time, when I didn't have so many other obligations, to serve the Lord? Why didn't I give myself totally to Him then?'"

Instead of rushing foolishly into a marriage because of impatience or one day reviewing our season of singleness with regret, let's commit to using our singleness to its fullest potential. Singleness is a gift. Let's rejoice in it and enjoy its opportunities today. Let's practice trusting God by pursuing His kingdom and His righteousness with all our hearts and by leaving the planning to Him.

In this life we will not understand all He does. But we know in the end, His perfect timing will be revealed. In a poem titled "Sometime," May Riley Smith beautifully expresses the perspective of heaven we will one day possess:

> Sometime, when all life's lessons have been learned,
> And sun and stars forevermore have set,
> The things which our weak judgments here have spurned,
> The things o'er which we grieved with lashes wet,
> Will flash before us out of life's dark night,
> As stars shine most in deeper tints of blue;
> And we shall see how all God's plans are right,
> And how what seemed reproof was love most true.

Then be content poor heart;
God's plans, like lilies pure and white, unfold;
we must not tear the close-shut leaves apart,—
Time will reveal the chalices of gold.
And if, through patient toil, we reach the land
Where tired feet, with sandals loosed, may rest,
When we shall clearly see and understand,
I think that we will say, "God knew the best!"

Do you believe that God knows best? Then place your life's calendar at His feet and allow Him to handle the scheduling of your relationships. Trust Him even if it means not dating when other people think you should. When God knows you're ready for the responsibility of commitment, He'll reveal the right person under the right circumstances.

"For I know the plans I have for you," God says matter-of-factly, "plans to prosper you and not to harm you, plans to give you hope and a future" (Jeremiah 29:11–13). Let's live our *todays* for His kingdom and entrust our *tomorrows* to His providence. We couldn't lay our futures in better hands. All we have to do is trust.

CHAPTER SIX

The Direction of Purity

HOW TO GET ON THE ROAD TO RIGHTEOUSNESS

While in high school I attended a weekend church retreat in which we discussed the topic of sexual purity. During one session our pastor asked all of us students to anonymously fill out survey cards that would let him know "how far" kids in the group had gone physically. He provided a rough scale for us to use, assigning numbers to levels of physical intimacy based on their seriousness. The activities ranged from light kissing at number one to sexual intercourse at number ten. Our pastor asked us to write down the highest number we had reached.

After dropping my card into a basket, I filed out of the classroom with two friends. I'll never forget the ensuing conversation. One of my buddies looked over at the other and said with a wink, "So how high did you score, man?"

Laughing, my other friend said he had reached eight, almost nine. Then these two guys proceeded to name the particular girls in the youth group with whom they had reached certain numbers.

FLIRTING WITH DARKNESS

My two friends exemplify how clouded our understanding of purity has become these days. We esteem purity too little and desire it too late. Even when we try to assert its importance, we render our words meaningless by our contradictory actions.

Do we desire purity in our relationships? We say we do. But do we live the kind of lives that foster this purity? Unfortunately, not often enough. "Make me chaste," prayed Augustine, "but not yet." Like him, we often have pricked consciences but unchanged lives. If we were honest with ourselves, many of us would admit that we're not really interested in purity at all. Instead, we feel satisfied by meeting the minimum requirements, content with spending our time in the "gray areas," flirting with darkness and never daring to step into the light of righteousness.

Like countless Christians, my two friends foolishly viewed purity and impurity as separated by a fixed point. As long as they didn't cross the line and go *all the way,* they believed they were still pure. True purity, however, is a direction, a persistent, determined pursuit of righteousness. This direction starts in the heart, and we express it in a lifestyle that flees opportunities for compromise.

ONE LITTLE STEP AT A TIME

If we truly seek to live pure lives, we can't allow ourselves to detour from the pursuit of righteousness for even a second. A story from the life of King David shows how dangerous such a detour can be. Few stories in the Bible fill me with as much dread as the story of David's fall into sin with Bathsheba. If a righteous man like David could fall into adultery and murder, who on earth can claim to be safe from temptation?

David walked in an intimacy of communion with God few have known. As a shepherd boy and as the king of God's people, he wrote the psalms—praises and petitions that encourage and inspire Christians to this day. David reveled in his Creator, worshiped Him, trusted Him, and enjoyed Him. God Himself called David a "man after my own heart" (Acts 13:22).

How could a man with such credentials descend so deep into sin and impurity?

One little step at a time.

David's plunge into sin didn't occur in a single leap. Like every journey into sin, David's journey into iniquity began with an almost imperceptible movement *away* from God.

When we first notice David's slide toward sin, we see him on the rooftop of his palace, but he had created the context for his misstep through an earlier decision. It was the spring of the new year, when kings led their armies to battle. But this year, David didn't go to the battlefield with his army. Instead, he stayed home. The choice may have been trivial, even justifiable, but the fact is that David was not where he was *supposed to be*— he was not on the front lines fighting God's battles.

Was this sin? Not blatantly, but it was a small step away from God's plan.

You may have heard people say that idleness is the devil's workshop, and so it was for David. The energy he should have exerted on the battlefield needed an outlet. Restless, he paced the palace rooftop. From there he caught sight of a woman bathing. Instead of averting his gaze, he indulged his desires and looked.

Another step.

Why did he continue to watch? He had seen the female body before, having married many times. But he coveted. Sin came in the form of a thought—David desired that which did not belong to him. Instead of rejecting the vileness of this thought, he entertained it, letting it linger in his mind.

If you're like every other human being, you've faced such a moment as this. Dwelling on the pros and cons of bowing to temptation, you have to make a choice. Will you or will you not stay within God's clear boundaries?

At this point in David's story, he could have stopped his journey toward sin. Instead, his hesitating steps down the path quickened into a run. He allowed lust to take control. David acted on his wicked imaginings, sent for Bathsheba, and slept with her.

The innocent shepherd was now an adulterer.

Complications arose. Bathsheba sent a message that she was pregnant. Her husband had been away from home for some time—he could not have fathered the child. Surely Bathsheba's husband, perhaps the whole nation, would discover her and David's impropriety. In haste and panic, David attempted to cover up the sin, but his attempts failed. Fearing certain scandal, David signed a letter that sealed the death of Bathsheba's husband, one of David's most loyal soldiers.

The psalmist was now a murderer.

How did David, this man after God's own heart, become an adulterer and murderer? When did he cross the line of purity? Was it the moment he touched Bathsheba or when he kissed her? Did it happen the moment he saw her bathing and chose to watch instead of turn away? Where did purity end and impurity begin?

As you can see from David's story, impurity isn't something we step into suddenly. It happens when we lose our focus on God. Often in dating relationships, impurity starts long before the moments of passion in back seats. Instead it begins in our hearts, in our motivations and attitudes. "I tell you that anyone who looks at a woman lustfully has already committed adultery with her in his heart," Jesus plainly states (Matthew 5:28). Sin begins in our minds and hearts.

We have to understand purity as a *pursuit* of righteousness. When we view it merely as a line, what keeps us from going as close as we can to the edge? If sex is the line, what's the difference between holding someone's hand and making out with that person? If kissing is the line, what's the difference between a goodnight peck and fifteen minutes of passionate lip-lock?

If we truly want to pursue purity, then we need to point ourselves in God's direction. We cannot simultaneously explore the boundaries of purity and pursue righteousness—they point us in opposite directions. True purity flees as fast and as far as it can from sin and compromise.

HEART AND PATH

If we want to lead pure lives, then we must realize that purity does not happen by accident. Rather, we must constantly pursue the direction of purity. The Book of Proverbs shows us that this ongoing process involves two things—our hearts and our feet.

In the Book of Proverbs, the seductive spirit of impurity and compromise is symbolized by a wayward adulteress. We are warned that "Many are the victims she has brought down; her slain are a mighty throng" (Proverbs 7:26). Though King Solomon wrote these words hundreds of years ago, this "woman" continues to lurk all around us today. She snares the innocent with promises of pleasure, but she truly desires nothing but her victims' destruction. She has ruined countless lives—both male and female—with her treachery.

Throughout history she has crippled the righteous. "Her house," the Bible solemnly warns, "is a highway to the grave, leading down to the chambers of death" (Proverbs 7:27). No matter how good impurity's victims may be, or how holy they've been in the past, if they set foot in her house, they speed toward death on an expressway with no exits. Have you ever made a wrong turn onto a freeway only to find you must travel many miles before you can get off to turn around? If so, you've probably felt the aggravation of your mistake. You can't slow down; you can't turn around; you can only continue speeding farther and farther from your destination. How many Christians in dating relationships have felt the same way as they struggle with accelerating physical involvement? They want to exit, but their own sinful passion takes them further and further from God's will.

How do you avoid the "on ramp" of impurity? How do you escape the spirit of adultery? Here's the answer: "Do not let your heart turn to her ways or stray into her paths" (Proverbs 7:25). Living a pure life before God requires the teamwork of your heart and your feet. The direction of purity begins within; you must support it in practical everyday decisions of where, when, and with whom you choose to be. Many couples have made commitments to sexual purity, but instead of adopting a lifestyle that supports this commitment, they continue relationships that encourage physical expression and place themselves in dangerous settings. The path you take with your feet should never contradict the conviction of your heart.

PURITY IN ACTION

If we desire purity, we have to fight for it. This means adjusting our attitudes and changing our lifestyles. The following pointers will help us maintain a direction of purity with both our hearts and our feet.

1. *Respect the deep significance of physical intimacy.*
We will never understand God's demand for sexual purity until we appreciate the deep spiritual and emotional implications of physical intimacy.

Many non-Christians view sex as a bodily function on the level of scratching another person's back. They engage in sex whenever and with whomever they want. While this lifestyle is an affront to biblical values, many Christians treat lesser expressions of physical intimacy with the same lack of respect. They view kissing, holding, or fondling another person as no big deal. While we may hold higher standards than our pagan neighbors, I'm afraid we, too, have lost sight of the deeper significance of sexual intimacy.

"Men tend to see the physical as more of an experience," a good female friend once told me. A girl's point of view is very different, she explained. "Kissing and 'making out' mean something very precious and deep to a woman," she said. "It is our way of giving our trust, our love, our heart to the man we love. It leaves us very vulnerable."

Physical intimacy is much more than two bodies colliding. God designed our sexuality as a physical expression of the oneness of marriage. God guards it carefully and places many stipulations on it because He considers it extremely precious. A man and woman who commit their lives to each other in marriage gain the *right* to express themselves sexually to each other. A husband and wife may enjoy each other's bodies because they in essence belong to each other. But if you're not married to someone, you have no claim on that person's body, no right to sexual intimacy.

Maybe you agree with this and plan to save sex for marriage. But in your opinion, you view "making out" activities such as kissing, necking, and fondling as no big deal. But we need to ask ourselves a serious question. If another person's body doesn't belong to us (that is, we're not married), what right do we have to treat the people we date any differently than a married person would treat someone who wasn't his or her spouse?

"But," you might say, "that's completely different." Is it really? Our culture has programmed us to think that singleness grants us license to fool around, to try out people emotionally and sexually. Since we're not married to anyone in particular, we can do what we want with anyone in general.

God has a very different view. "Honor marriage, and guard the sacredness of sexual intimacy between wife and husband," He commands (Hebrews 13:4, *The Message*).

This honor for the sacredness of sexuality between husband and wife starts *now*, not just after the wedding day. Respect for the institution of marriage should motivate us to protect it from violation while we're single. We can do this by recognizing the deep significance of sexual intimacy—at *any* level—and refusing to steal these privileges before marriage.

2. Set your standards too high.

In the early days of his ministry, Billy Graham experienced deep concern over the public's distrust of evangelists. How could he preach the gospel to people who assumed he was a fake? As he considered this question, he realized that most people who distrusted evangelists did so because those evangelists lacked integrity, particularly in the area of sexuality. To combat this, he and the close circle of men who ran the crusades avoided opportunities to be alone with women who weren't their wives.

Think about this for a moment. What an inconvenience! Did these men really fear that they'd commit adultery the moment they found themselves alone with a woman? Weren't they going a little too far?

We'll let history answer the question for us. In the last fifty years, what has shaken and demoralized the church as much as the immorality of Christian leaders? What believer can hold his head high when the scandalous conduct of many televangelists is mentioned? But even unbelievers honor the name of Billy Graham. Mr. Graham has earned the respect of the world by his faithfulness and his integrity. How did Billy Graham do this when so many others failed? He set his standards too high—he went above and beyond the call of righteousness.

We can only attain righteousness by doing two things—destroying sin in its embryonic stage and fleeing temptation. Mr. Graham did both. He cut off the opportunity for sin at its root, and he fled from even the possibility of compromise.

God calls us to the same zeal for righteousness in premarital relationships. What exactly does that look like? For me and many other people I know, it has meant rejecting typical dating. I go out with groups of friends; I avoid one-on-one dating because it encourages physical intimacy and places me in an isolated setting with a girl. Can't I handle it? Don't I have any self-control? Yeah, maybe I could handle it, but that's not the point. God says, "Flee the evil desires of youth, and pursue righteousness, faith, love and peace, along with those who call on the Lord out of a pure heart" (2 Timothy 2:22). I won't stick around to see how much temptation I can take. God is not impressed with my ability to stand up to sin. He's more impressed by the obedience I show when I run from it.

For couples moving toward engagement or those already engaged, the same principle applies. Set your standards higher

than you need to. Cut off sin at its root. Until you're married—
and I mean until you've walked down that aisle and exchanged
vows—don't act as if your bodies belong to each other.

Maybe you think I'm taking this idea too far. Maybe you're
saying, "You've got to be joking. One little kiss won't have me
hurtling toward certain sin." Let me encourage you to give this
idea a little more thought. For just a moment, consider the possibility that even the most innocent form of sexual expression
outside of marriage could be dangerous.

Let me explain why I believe this. Physical interaction
encourages us to start something we're not supposed to finish,
awakening desires we're not allowed to consummate, turning
on passions we have to turn off. What foolishness! The Bible
tells us the path of sin, particularly in regard to the wrong use
of our sexuality, is like a highway to the grave. We shouldn't get
on it then try to stop before we arrive at the destination—God
tells us to stay off that highway completely.

God designed our sexuality to operate within the protection
and commitment of marriage. God made sex to end in full con-
summation. Every step along the path of pure sexuality—from
an initial glance between husband and wife to a kiss—potentially leads toward physical oneness. In marriage, things are
supposed to progress—things are allowed to get "out of hand."

And I really believe that before marriage we can't keep from
abusing God's gift of sex unless we choose to stay off the path
altogether. In Colossians 3:5 we read, "Put to death, therefore,
whatever belongs to your earthly nature: sexual immorality,
impurity, lust, evil desires..." Tolerated sin is pampered sin—it
grows and gains strength. James tells us that "each one is tempted
when, by his own evil desire, he is dragged away and enticed.
Then, after desire has conceived, it gives birth to sin; and sin,
when it is full-grown, gives birth to death" (James 1:14–15). If

we begin the progression of sin and allow it to continue, it will soon grow beyond our control. Only by keeping our standards too high and killing sin in its infantile stage will we avoid its destruction.

Set your standards too high. You will never regret purity.

3. *Make the purity of others a priority.*
One of the best ways to maintain a pure life is to watch out for the purity of others. What can you do to protect your brothers and sisters in the Lord from impurity? What can you say to encourage them to keep their hearts set in the direction of righteousness?

The support and protection you can provide to same-sex friends is important, but the protection you can give to opposite-sex friends is invaluable. When it comes to purity in relationships—both physical and emotional—girls and guys usually trip each other up. Can you imagine the righteousness that could be born if both sexes took it upon themselves to watch out for each other?

Let's look at specific ways this can be accomplished.

The Guy's Responsibility
Guys, it's time we stood up to defend the honor and righteousness of our sisters. We need to stop acting like "hunters" trying to catch girls and begin seeing ourselves as warriors standing guard over them.

How do we do this? First we must realize that girls don't struggle with the same temptations we struggle with. We wrestle more with our sex drives while girls struggle more with their emotions. We can help guard their hearts by being sincere and honest in our communication. We need to swear off flirtatiousness and refuse to play games and lead them on. We have to go out of our way to make sure nothing we say or do stirs up inappropriate feelings or expectations.

A good friend, Matt Canlis, modeled this idea of guarding a girl's purity in his relationship with Julie Clifton, the woman to whom he's now married. Long before they began pursuing marriage, both felt deeply attracted to the other. But during a certain season, God made it clear to Julie that she had to focus on Him and not be distracted by Matt.

Although Matt didn't know this at the time, he made it his priority to guard Julie's heart during this time of waiting, even though he felt personally drawn to her. Matt controlled his desire to flirt with Julie. He passed up opportunities to spend time alone with her, and when they were in group settings he refrained from singling her out and focusing too much attention on her. He avoided doing anything that would make it harder for Julie to focus on serving God.

This season didn't last forever, and eventually Matt and Julie became engaged. I had lunch with both of them a few weeks before their wedding. Julie explained how grateful she felt that Matt had enough maturity to put her needs above his own. By making her emotional and spiritual purity a priority, Matt helped Julie focus her mind and heart on God. If Matt had acted selfishly, he could have distracted Julie and ruined what God wanted to accomplish in and through her life.

What an example of brotherly love! I want to weep when I think of the many times I have neglected my responsibility to guard girls' hearts. Instead of playing the role of a warrior, I played the thief, stealing their focus from God for myself. I'm determined to do better. I want to be the kind of friend to whom girls' future husbands could one day say, "Thank you for standing watch over my wife's heart. Thank you for guarding her purity."

The Girl's Responsibility

Girls, you have an equally important role. Remember the wayward woman we discussed earlier? Your job is to keep your brothers from being led astray by her charms. Please be aware of how easily your actions and glances can stir up lust in a guy's mind.

You may not realize this, but we guys most commonly struggle with our eyes. I think many girls are innocently unaware of the difficulty a guy has in remaining pure when looking at a girl who is dressed immodestly. Now I don't want to dictate your wardrobe, but honestly speaking, I would be blessed if girls considered more than fashion when shopping for clothes. Yes, guys are responsible for maintaining self-control, but you can help by refusing to wear clothing designed to attract attention to your body.

I know the world tells you that if you have a nice body, you should show it off. And we men have only helped feed this mentality. But I think you can play a part in reversing this trend. I know many girls who would look great in shorter skirts or tighter blouses, and they know it. But they choose to dress modestly. They take the responsibility of guarding their brothers' eyes. To these women and others like them, I'm grateful.

"And let us consider how we may spur one another on toward love and good deeds" (Hebrews 10:24). It's time to start seeing other people's purity as our responsibility.

THE BEAUTY OF PURITY

In closing, let me ask you this: Can you picture it? Can you see the beauty of purity? And if you can, will you fight for it in your own life as well as in the lives of others?

Yes, it requires work. Purity doesn't happen by accident; it requires obedience to God. But this obedience is not burdensome or overbearing. We have only to consider the alternatives to impurity to see the beauty of walking in God's will. Impurity is a grimy film that coats the soul, a shadow that blocks light and darkens our countenance. God's love for the impure does not cease, but their ability to enjoy this love does. For in our impurity we are turned from Him. Sin and its defilement are never found near His throne—they can only gain advantage when we turn away from His radiance.

Turned from God's presence we are completely unprotected from the marauding destruction of sin. Without purity, God's gift of sexuality becomes a dangerous game. A relationship devoid of purity is soon reduced to nothing more than two bodies grasping at and demanding pleasure. Without purity, the mind becomes a slave to depravity, tossed about by every sinful craving and imagination.

What will it take for us to see the beauty of purity? Purity is the entrance to the splendor of God's creation. "Who may ascend the hill of the LORD? Who may stand in his holy place? He who has clean hands and a pure heart..." (Psalm 24:3–4). Purity ushers us into God's presence. "Blessed are the pure in heart," Christ said, "for they will see God" (Matthew 5:8). Only the pure may see His face. Only the pure may be vessels of His Holy Spirit.

Do you see the beauty and power and protection of purity? Do you want all this? Do you ache for it? Are you ready to deny yourself the pleasures of the moment to live a pure, God-focused life? May your love for Him fuel a lifelong, passionate pursuit of righteousness.

CHAPTER SEVEN

A Cleansed Past: The Room

HOW JESUS CAN REDEEM YOUR PAST

I don't usually share my dreams with people, but I'd like to tell you about a particularly stirring one I once had.

As Christians, we "know" certain things such as "Jesus loves me" and "Christ died for sinners." We've heard these statements countless times, but the dust of familiarity can dim the glory of these simple truths. We have to brush them off and remind ourselves of their life-transforming power.

A dream I had one humid night while visiting a pastor in Puerto Rico was one such reminder. It summed up what Jesus Christ did for me and for you.

I share it here because after a chapter on the importance of striving for purity, we need a reminder of God's grace. For some, myself included, a discussion of purity is an exercise in regret—it reminds us of our impurity and the times we've failed.

Maybe you've blown it. Maybe you reflect on past actions and wince with remorse. Purity seems like a lost cause. This dream, called "The Room," is dedicated to you.

In that place between wakefulness and dreams, I found myself in the room. There were no distinguishing features save for the one wall covered with small index-card files. They were like the ones in libraries that list titles by author or subject in alphabetical order. But these files, which stretched from floor to ceiling and seemingly endless in either direction, had very different headings. As I drew near the wall of files, the first to catch my attention was one that read "Girls I Have Liked." I opened it and began flipping through the cards. I quickly shut it, shocked to realize that I recognized the names written on each one.

And then without being told, I knew exactly where I was. This lifeless room with its small files was a crude catalog system for my life. Here were written the actions of my every moment, big and small, in a detail my memory couldn't match.

A sense of wonder and curiosity, coupled with horror, stirred within me as I began randomly opening files and exploring their contents. Some brought joy and sweet memories; others a sense of shame and regret so intense that I would look over my shoulder to see if anyone was watching. A file named "Friends" was next to one marked "Friends I Have Betrayed."

The titles ranged from the mundane to the outright weird. "Books I Have Read," "Lies I Have Told," "Comfort I Have Given," "Jokes I Have Laughed At." Some were almost hilarious in their exactness: "Things I've Yelled at My Brothers." Others I couldn't laugh at: "Things I Have Done in Anger," "Things I Have Muttered under My Breath at My Parents." I never ceased to be surprised by the contents. Often there were many more cards than I expected. Sometimes there were fewer than I hoped.

I was overwhelmed by the sheer volume of the life I had lived. Could it be possible that I had the time in my twenty years to write each of these thousands, possibly millions, of cards? But each card confirmed this truth. Each was written in my own handwriting. Each signed with my signature.

When I pulled out the file marked "Songs I Have Listened To," I realized the files grew to contain their contents. The cards were packed tightly, and yet after two or three yards, I hadn't found the end of the file. I shut it, shamed, not so much by the quality of music, but more by the vast amount of time I knew that file represented.

When I came to a file marked "Lustful Thoughts," I felt a chill run through my body. I pulled the file out only an inch, not willing to test its size, and drew out a card. I shuddered at its detailed contents. I felt sick to think that such a moment had been recorded.

Suddenly I felt an almost animal rage. One thought dominated my mind: "No one must ever see these cards! No one must ever see this room! I have to destroy them!" In an insane frenzy I yanked the file out. Its size didn't matter now. I had to empty it and burn the cards. But as I took the file at one end and began pounding it on the floor, I could not dislodge a single card. I became desperate and pulled out a card, only to find it as strong as steel when I tried to tear it.

Defeated and utterly helpless, I returned the file to its slot. Leaning my forehead against the wall, I let out a long, self-pitying sigh. And then I saw it. The title bore

"People I Have Shared the Gospel With." The handle was brighter than those around it, newer, almost unused. I pulled on its handle and a small box not more than three inches long fell into my hands. I could count the cards it contained on one hand.

And then the tears came. I began to weep. Sobs so deep that they hurt started in my stomach and shook through me. I fell on my knees and cried. I cried out of shame, from the overwhelming shame of it all. The rows of file shelves swirled in my tear-filled eyes. No one must ever, ever know of this room. I must lock it up and hide the key.

But then as I pushed away the tears, I saw Him. No, please not Him. Not here. Oh, anyone but Jesus.

I watched helplessly as He began to open the files and read the cards. I couldn't bear to watch His response. And in the moments I could bring myself to look at His face, I saw a sorrow deeper than my own. He seemed to intuitively go to the worst boxes. Why did He have to read every one?

Finally He turned and looked at me from across the room. He looked at me with pity in His eyes. But this was a pity that didn't anger me. I dropped my head, covered my face with my hands and began to cry again. He walked over and put His arm around me. He could have said so many things. But He didn't say a word. He just cried with me.

Then He got up and walked back to the wall of files. Starting at one end of the room, He took out a file and, one by one, began to sign His name over mine on each card.

"No!" I shouted, rushing to Him. All I could find to

say was "No, no," as I pulled the card from Him. His name shouldn't be on these cards. But there it was, written in red so rich, so dark, so alive. The name of Jesus covered mine. It was written with His blood.

He gently took the card back. He smiled a sad smile and continued to sign the cards. I don't think I'll ever understand how He did it so quickly, but the next instant it seemed I heard Him close the last file and walk back to my side. He placed His hand on my shoulder and said, "It is finished."

I stood up, and He led me out of the room. There was no lock on its door. There were still cards to be written.

For sinners like you and me, there's good news: Christ paid our debt. He has covered our sin with His blood; He has forgotten the past. Purity starts today.

"So let us put aside the deeds of darkness and put on the armor of light" (Romans 13:12). Admittedly some will have more to lay aside than others—more memories, more pain, more regrets. But the past needn't determine our future. We have choices right now about how we'll live. Will we set our hearts on God and walk in His paths? "Let us behave decently," the passage in Romans continues, "...not in sexual immorality and debauchery...Rather, clothe yourselves with the Lord Jesus Christ, and do not think about how to gratify the desires of the sinful nature" (Romans 13:13–14).

Not one of us can stand completely pure before God. We are all sinners. But no matter how filthy the rags of our defilement may be, in a moment of true surrender the heart turned toward God loses its impurity. God clothes us in Christ's righteousness. He no longer sees our sin. He transfers Jesus' purity to us. So see yourself as God sees you—clothed in radiant white, pure, justified.

Maybe you have a particular memory that continues to hound you, a memory that makes you feel unworthy of God's love and forgiveness. Don't let the past beat you up. Forget it. Don't replay that moment or any others like it. If you've repented of all those behaviors, God has promised to remember them no more (Hebrews 8:12). Move on. A lifetime of purity awaits you.

PART THREE

Building a
New Lifestyle

CHAPTER EIGHT

Starting with a Clean Slate

FOUR IMPORTANT STEPS FOR GETTING ON TRACK WITH GOD'S PLAN

B uilding well sometimes means first tearing down.

Recently my dad and my younger brother Joel attended a birthday party for Stephen Taylor, one of Joel's best friends. It was a very special occasion. Stephen was turning thirteen, and his dad wanted to make Stephen's entrance into young adulthood memorable. Nice presents wouldn't suffice; Stephen's dad wanted to impart wisdom. To accomplish this he asked fathers to accompany their sons to the party and to bring a special gift—a tool that served them in their specific lines of work.

Each father gave his tool to Stephen along with its accompanying "life lesson" for the "toolbox" of principles Stephen would carry into life. The tools were as unique as the men who used them. My dad gave Stephen a quality writing pen and explained that a pen not only served him when he wrote his ideas but also represented his word when he signed an agreement.

During the gift giving, a father who was a professional home builder handed Stephen a small box. "Inside that box is the tool I use most," he said. Stephen opened it and found a nail puller.

"My nail puller, simple as it might seem," the father explained, "is one of the most important tools I have." This father told the story of how once, while in the middle of building a wall, he discovered that it was crooked. Instead of halting the construction and undoing a little work to fix the wall, he decided to proceed, hoping that the problem would go away as he continued to build. However, the problem only worsened. Eventually, at a great loss of materials and time, he had to tear down the nearly completed wall and totally rebuild it.

"Stephen," the father said gravely, "times will come in life when you'll realize you've made a mistake. At that moment, you have two choices: You can swallow your pride and 'pull a few nails,' or you can foolishly continue your course, hoping the problem will go away. Most of the time the problem will only get worse. I'm giving you this tool to remind you of this principle: When you realize you've made a mistake, the best thing you can do is tear it down and start over."

BUILDING A GODLY LIFESTYLE

The lesson of the nail puller is an important one for all of us who have built our relationships on the faulty attitudes and patterns of dating. For many, getting things right will require us to first tear down what's wrong. In some cases, that means bringing wrong relationships to an end.

Whatever your circumstances, the following steps are important for starting and maintaining a lifestyle of godliness in relationships.

1. *Start with a clean slate.*
If we want to build a godly lifestyle, we must first repent of sinful attitudes and behaviors in our relationships. The Bible uses

the word *repent* to describe turning from what's wrong and pursuing what's right. Repentance is a change of direction based on a change of heart.

Have you practiced selfishness in relationships? If so, consider admitting your selfishness and correcting it. Have you played loose and careless in the area of purity? Then maybe you need to ask God to forgive you and seek ways to reverse your course. Are you currently involved in a relationship that you know is wrong, for whatever reason? Then ask God to give you the courage to do His will, which might include breaking off the relationship.

Breaking Up Is Hard to Do

Danny, an eighteen-year-old, knew that he could fix the problems in his relationship with Trisha by doing only one thing: ending the relationship. They had dated for over seven months, and during that time, they had quickly escalated their physical involvement. They didn't mean to, but no matter how many times they made rules about where to stop, they always went further. Neither was ready to get married, and deep down Danny really didn't believe he and Trisha were right for each other anyway. Continuing the relationship with Trisha would only mislead her.

Did any of these factors make breaking up easy? No, this messy aspect of relationships will always be hard. But remember, continuing a wrong relationship only increases the pain when it finally does end. Have the courage to obey now. Obedience today will save you a lot of sorrow and regret tomorrow.

When you end a relationship, you need to remember a couple of important things. First, really end it. Don't leave any strings attached or hint at the possibility of reuniting someday. You should also probably agree to steer clear of each other for a while afterward. In Danny's case, he felt tempted to call Trisha after their breakup "just to chat" or to ask her to go out "just for old time's sake." But doing so would only reawaken old feelings and open old wounds. Though it wasn't easy, he knew that he and Trisha had to end the relationship with finality.

Adjusting the Focus of a Relationship

One day Sheena realized that a relationship with one of her guy friends from church was becoming more and more serious. They weren't dating, but they always seemed to end up together in groups, and they talked on the phone quite often. Upon realizing this, Sheena decided to sit down with her friend and express her concern: "I really want to be friends with you, but I think we focus a little too much time on each other." Though Sheena struggled to muster the nerve to say this, that little conversation helped keep the friendship on the right track.

Starting with a clean slate doesn't always involve a breakup. Sometimes it simply means refocusing a relationship to keep it from heading in the wrong direction.

Be Humble

When Jonathan broke up with Kara, he didn't try to point out how she shared the blame for problems in their relationship. "That wouldn't have been apologizing," he said. Instead, he asked her to forgive him for being the one to push the physical side of their relationship. "I told her I'd been a terrible example of a Christian and that breaking up was what I believed God wanted me to do."

Whether you're having to break up or refocus a relationship, approach the other person humbly, stressing your desire to please God. If you've wronged that person, confess your guilt and ask for forgiveness. Don't rationalize or make excuses. Just apologize.

2. *Make your parents your teammates.*

You'll need two things as you live out a new attitude toward relationships: wisdom and accountability. Ideally, both of these should come from your parents. You need your mom and dad. (I realize that not everyone has the opportunity to benefit from relationships with both parents, but even so, I believe that you can gain valuable insight from whichever parent or guardian you most trust.)

Why do I say we need to gain wisdom and accountability from our parents? Because I can see how I shot myself in the foot by *not* trusting my parents in the past. When I was in high school, I hid my relationships from my parents. If I liked someone, I wouldn't let my parents know. I feared that if they got involved they'd mess things up. What a mistake! By hiding my romantic life from my parents, I cut myself off from the God-given source of wisdom that could have saved me from making so many mistakes.

I've spent the last several years learning to be open and honest with my parents about my romantic interests. And as I've done this, I've made an incredible discovery: My mom and dad are on my side! What a relief to tell them what I'm going through! These conversations don't have to be embarrassing or confrontational. I just go to my parents and say, "I've been thinking about so-and-so. What do you guys think of her?" Or "I'm really distracted by this person. Would you pray for me?"

As I openly discuss my thoughts and feelings with my parents, they can remind me of the commitments I've made (a pretty girl can so easily make me forget them!). They can also provide prayer and counsel. But they can't do this unless I choose to actively involve them and seek their wisdom. I've gained some wonderful insights as I've done this, and I think you could, too. I challenge you to make your parents your teammates.

When Dad and Mom Aren't Around

As I mentioned earlier, I realize that some people just don't have the option to involve their parents in this way. Maybe your parents are divorced, non-Christians, or just completely uninterested in being involved. Or you may be living away from home.

If you're in one of these situations, please understand that God can provide all the support you need. He does this through His Holy Spirit and through the lives of other Christians in your local church. If you need to find a mentor who will give you wisdom and accountability regarding your relationships, ask God to show you who to turn to. Then, when He brings a mentor into your life, actively invite that person's input. If you're not already involved in a church, find one and ask a godly older man or woman there to fill the role of adopted dad or mom as you navigate the sea of romantic relationships.

Whatever your circumstances, don't procrastinate. Develop a support team to help you stay on track.

3. Establish protective boundaries.

After you've formed your "team," you need to establish boundaries and guidelines for your relationships with the opposite sex. Sit down with your mom and dad or mentor, and ask questions such as "What constitutes a romantic setting? When is going out with someone appropriate, and when would it lead to premature intimacy?" Think through some of the situations that might arise. What do you do when someone feels attracted to you or vice versa? How much time should you spend on the phone with someone of the opposite sex? How much time should you spend together, even in group settings?

Setting boundaries like these will allow you to respond with confidence in different situations. For example, I have committed to avoiding situations that could lead to temptation. For me, being alone with a girl in an empty house is one such situation. So I've created a boundary about this issue: I will not go to a girl's home if no one else is there. If a girl calls me, invites me to come over, and mentions in passing that her parents aren't home, I don't have to weigh the situation or pray about it—I already know that I won't accept the invitation.

Rules by themselves won't change our hearts, but once we've taken on a new attitude, protective boundaries can help keep us on course.

4. *Check who's whispering in your ear.*

Finally, keep an eye on your influences. Who and what you listen to, read, and watch will either encourage or conflict with your commitment to pursue God's best in relationships.

I remember talking to a girl at my church who commented on how dissatisfied she felt after watching romantic movies. "It makes me wonder, 'Why doesn't that happen to me?'" she said.

Does anything in your life cause that kind of discontentment? If so, then maybe you need to consider cutting out some things. Maybe you need to stop reading romance novels and watching soap operas because they encourage ungodly longings within you. Perhaps you need to turn off the radio because much of today's music exalts a false definition of love. You might need to tune out some of your favorite TV shows because they mock your beliefs about purity. Whatever even tempts you toward discontent or compromise, don't put up with it. Tune it out. Turn it off.

You may find that a similar principle applies to spending too much time with friends who are obsessed with the dating scene. I'm not saying that you should dump your friends because they encourage you to dwell on dating, but I do think you should be aware of how your friends affect your thoughts. Ask yourself these questions: Are these people negatively affecting me? How can I be a positive influence on them without compromising my convictions? The answer might involve spending less time with certain people or choosing to spend time with them in different settings. Pray for these friends and love them, but honestly assess their influence on you. And ask God to bring people into your life who will provide support for your standards and beliefs.

LET'S LIVE IT

The pastor A. W. Tozer once preached a particularly convicting sermon to his congregation. One person who heard it recalls that, had he so desired, Tozer could have filled the altar with a repentant, sobbing throng. But Tozer wasn't interested in a display of emotion. Instead of delivering an altar call, Tozer told his congregation to quietly leave the service. "Don't come down here and cry about it," he boomed. "Go home and live it!"

Tozer's instruction is perfect for us. Though they might seem difficult at first, the four steps we've examined in this chapter are a vital part of building a new lifestyle. They will not only help us start strong, but even more important, they can help us follow through—to "go home and live" what's right.

We can take our first step by refocusing relationships headed off course or ending those we know are wrong. To embrace all the good God has in store for us, we need to let go of past sin and mistakes. We also need a team—parents and other godly friends—who can keep us accountable and provide encouragement. Let's be humble enough to invite their correction and counsel. And let's be honest enough to admit we need protective boundaries in our lives to keep us far from temptation and compromise. Finally, let's honestly evaluate the influence of what we watch, what we listen to, and who we hang out with. Actively following the four steps in this chapter will help us put our convictions into action.

Yes, we'll still face many questions. How can we have friendships with the opposite sex without becoming romantic? What do we do when attracted to or even infatuated with someone? And how can we explain "not dating" to those around us? We'll look at these and many other issues in the next three chapters.

CHAPTER NINE

Just Friends in a Just-Do-It World

KEYS FOR KEEPING YOUR RELATIONSHIPS WITH THE OPPOSITE SEX OUT OF THE "ROMANTIC ZONE"

Y ou meet someone of the opposite sex. He or she really catches your eye.

Uh-oh.

Then you get to know this person, and you find out he or she has a great personality as well.

Double uh-oh.

To top it all off, this person sends you that "I'd like to get to know you better" vibe.

Major uh-oh!

If you've decided to put romance on hold until you're ready for marriage, what do you do in a situation like this? If you're not going to play the dating game, what's the plan?

The simple answer is to just be friends. Easy, right? Not quite. Maybe we wouldn't struggle with this scenario if God created us without hearts, devoid of emotions, and immune to attraction. But He didn't. Most of us have to deal with all three as we stumble through the confusing process of finding balance between two extreme options: jumping headlong into romance with everyone who catches our eye or running in fear from all members of the opposite sex. Finding that balance is anything but easy. The middle ground can often feel more like a tightrope stretched over a gaping chasm.

Just Plain Confusing

Being "just friends" is just plain confusing. In all honesty, I haven't completely figured it out. Romance runs in my veins, and it's not always easy to restrain. Even when I want to maintain a platonic relationship with a girl, I struggle with keeping myself from stepping into something more.

Where is the line between friendship and "more than friendship," anyway? Trying to answer that question reminds me of a Tootsie Pop commercial I watched as a kid. Maybe you've seen it. A little boy has a Tootsie Pop and a very valid question: How many licks does it take to get to the middle of a Tootsie Roll-filled lollipop?

He asks a couple of animals his question, but nobody knows the answer. They direct him to the owl. The owl would know; owls are smart.

So the boy poses his question to the owl, who sits in his tree like some mountaintop guru: "How many licks does it take to get to the chewy center of a Tootsie Pop?"

The owl thoughtfully takes the sucker and removes the wrapping.

He licks once. "One," he counts.

He licks again. "Two," he says.

He licks a third time. "Three."

And suddenly, crunch! Throwing patience to the wind, the owl bites into the middle of the Tootsie Pop. Handing the bare Tootsie Pop stick to the boy, the owl announces his answer to the mystifying question: "Three."

That owl made me so mad when I was a kid. I felt sorry for

the boy. Not only did he lose his Tootsie Pop, but he still didn't know the true answer to his question.

When I consider friendship with girls, I feel like that boy! I don't want to reach the chewy center of romance—I just want to be friends. But I don't always know how much attention a friendship between a guy and girl can handle before— crunch!—we've crossed the line from friendship into "more than friendship."

I don't raise this concern because I'm afraid of romance. On the contrary, I look forward to one day growing to love a girl and doing my best to sweep her off her feet. But until that time comes, I want to focus on serving God in my singleness. To stay on this course, I've chosen to avoid dating, steering clear of any romantic entanglements.

But sometimes my friendships go "crunch!"

Have you ever realized that a friendship has tipped over into romance? If so, then you know how difficult it can be to avoid this situation. One moment you're pals, then all of a sudden your heart kicks into high gear. You sigh when you think of this person. You find yourself daydreaming of the next time you can spend time with this "friend." Or you're with a group of friends, and when that particular person talks with someone else you feel…something. Jealous? Possessive?

You try to reason with yourself. "Why would I feel this way? We're just friends. We're brother and sister in Christ…" You can say whatever you want, but you know deep down that you've "crunched."

FRIENDS FOREVER

To my shame I have a whole file of my own "crunch!" stories— friendships with girls complicated, and sometimes ruined, because we became romantic. I'll share one of these stories here to help show how "crunching" can progress.

At age seventeen, I had just gotten out of a serious, two-year relationship that had shown me firsthand the pitfalls of dating. While my former girlfriend was, and is, a wonderful person, we broke up with many regrets. But now I had a chance to start over, and I was determined to avoid the mistakes of the past. I developed a simple plan: Until I was ready for marriage and had found the right girl, I would just be friends with members of the opposite sex.

Easier said than done.

I had good intentions, but I set out with a naive understanding of the nature of guy-girl friendships. At this point in time, I thought friendship with a girl meant you didn't kiss her or officially date. I had a lot to learn.

With my limited understanding, I embarked on my new approach to friendships with girls. It didn't take long before I had a chance to test my ideas. I met Chelsea the summer before my senior year in high school. She was a fellow student at The Summit, a Christian leadership training camp held in a quaint but rickety turn-of-the-century hotel in Colorado Springs, Colorado. Chelsea and I met on the stairs one day between classes. She was a pretty brunette from Kansas who radiated wholesomeness. A strong Christian from a good family, Chelsea was as American as apple pie—athletic and adventurous. It was definitely a case of "like" at first sight.

Over the course of the camp we got to know each other, talking in the lunch line and playing tennis on sports days. We grew even closer when we and a group of students hiked fourteen miles to the top of Pikes Peak. During the trek, Chelsea told me about life in the small town where her dad practiced law. I told her about my life at home in Oregon. As we talked, I felt elated to have found a girl whose company I could enjoy without all the trappings of being boyfriend and girlfriend.

Unfortunately, my desire for "just friendship" wasn't as strong as my old habits of edging toward romance with girls. I felt attracted to Chelsea, and instead of being content with friendship and keeping our interaction in the context of a group, I asked her out to lunch. She accepted, and two days before camp ended, we rode the bus into downtown Colorado Springs. We spent the afternoon meandering through tourist traps full of knickknacks and cheap paintings. At a bead shop we made necklaces as reminders of each other.

This little date was Mistake Number One. In my opinion, going out to lunch isn't a big deal, but in this case it signaled my special interest in Chelsea, placed us in a romantically charged setting, and made us feel like a couple. My instigation of this interaction pushed our relationship beyond friendship.

But at the time, I was blind to all of this. In fact, I felt proud of myself. As far as I was concerned, Chelsea and I had been completely above reproach. Good grief! We hadn't so much as held hands! As "mature" high schoolers, we had risen above the junior high tendency to be boyfriend and girlfriend at camp then break up when we went home. We told ourselves and our friends at camp that we were just friends.

The truth, however, is that I grasped for more. I wanted the excitement of romance and the comfort of being liked. The next day, I wrote Chelsea a note saying that I couldn't bear to have the end of camp signal the end of our friendship. Even though we lived far apart, could we please keep in touch through the mail? She agreed.

This was Mistake Number Two. Now, letter writing is a fine thing. I wrote to several friends, both guys and girls, after camp. But Chelsea and I did more than keep in touch. For several months, we wrote each other almost every day. The relationship not only cost a small fortune in postage, it bordered on obsession. When I wasn't writing to Chelsea or poring over the letters she had written to me, I was thinking and talking about her.

To any rational person, we were obviously much more than friends. Even though we closed each letter with "Friends forever," these poetic missives dripped with romantic overtones. We scattered "I miss yous" and "I can't stop thinking about yous" heavily throughout each epistle. On one note Chelsea wrote, "I love you in Christ" in bright letters at the top of each page.

Just friends? Yeah, right.

As I look back, I'm amazed at how I justified my actions. "How can this be wrong?" I reasoned. "We live thousands of miles apart, have never kissed, and can't even date!" What I failed to realize is that you don't have to live next door to someone to pursue intimacy prematurely. And you don't have to go on dates to overstep the limits of friendship; the U.S. Postal Service allows you to accomplish this despite distance.

The relationship didn't end well. Chelsea and I became more serious. We even flew out to visit each other. But eventually we began to see that we had less in common than we had originally thought. Our romantic ardor had glossed over our incompatibilities.

When Chelsea met another guy from school and began being "just friends" with him, I became jealous. We couldn't evaluate our "friendship" objectively, we hurt each other's feelings, and eventually our letter writing died along with our relationship—another premature romance ended in heartbreak.

I had ended up in the same situation I had been so determined to avoid.

How did it happen? When did our friendship develop into

something more? Could I ever be just friends with a girl, or was it entirely impossible?

THE POSSIBILITIES OF GUY-GIRL FRIENDSHIPS

Though I've sometimes failed in my attempts to walk the fine line between friendship and romance with girls, I do believe guys and girls can have life-enriching, non-romantic friendships. In fact, it's important that we do. The apostle Paul instructs his spiritual son Timothy to treat younger women "as sisters, with absolute purity" (1 Timothy 5:2). Paul assumes that Timothy interacts with women daily, and because of this assumption, he exhorts Timothy to pursue a godly attitude and purity. We need to pursue these things as well.

Guy-girl friendships can be pure, inspiring, and educational. As I've interacted with female friends, I've gained insight into their perspective on life, learning valuable things I would have missed in my narrow-minded, male outlook. I remember getting a note from a female friend in which she listed several of her favorite passages of Scripture. I had been working on memorizing some verses, and when I looked up the verses this friend had listed, I realized that I had originally developed a lopsided memory plan. All my memory verses had to do with conquering the enemy, beating the devil, and overcoming temptation. Her verses focused on simple faith in God, servanthood, and trust in His goodness. Though she never knew it, her perspective on our heavenly Father helped balance my understanding of God.

Maybe you've gained something equally valuable from a friendship with a member of the opposite sex. This kind of friendship can help us see life from a different perspective. They have the potential to challenge us spiritually and encourage our growth.

THE ABUSE OF A HARMLESS THING

While we should take advantage of the benefits of guy-girl friendships, we must not forget their boundaries. If we want to enjoy anything good, we must recognize its limitations, and friendship with the opposite sex is no exception. No matter how beneficial or innocent something may be, when we ask too much of it, we can cause harm to ourselves and to others. Solomon passed down this principle using the analogy of food: "If you find honey, eat just enough—too much of it, and you will vomit" (Proverbs 25:16). Just because something is good doesn't mean we should gorge on it. Like healthy eating, healthy friendships require self-control and moderation.

Let's look at three important steps involved in maintaining healthy friendships with the opposite sex.

1. *Understand the difference between friendship and intimacy.*
We can more clearly see the elusive line between friendship and "more than friendship" when we understand the difference between friendship and intimacy.

Friendship is about something other than the two people in the relationship; intimacy is about each other. In a true friendship, something outside the two friends brings them together. C. S. Lewis writes, "We picture lovers face to face, but friends side by side; their eyes look ahead." The key to friendship is a common goal or object on which both companions focus. It can be an athletic pursuit, a hobby, faith, or music, but it's something *outside* of them. As soon as the two people involved focus on *the relationship,* it has moved beyond friendship.

Can you see how this progression took place in my story with Chelsea? In the beginning, we based our friendship on the fact that we were both at a leadership camp for two weeks. We shared other common interests such as tennis and the piano. Our interaction based on these things remained within the bounds of friendship.

But we had little reason to continue our friendship from a distance. We couldn't participate in common interests side by side over the miles. We had no basis for continuing the relationship except for the fact that we were interested in each other. If we had truly pursued friendship, we would have seen that our friendship couldn't transcend the limits of geography and lifestyle. We'd have admitted that the only thing bringing us together was common attraction.

But we didn't. Thus the focus of our correspondence moved from our common interests to our relationship. We turned from walking side by side to being face to face, focused on one another.

The reason that most guy-girl friendships cross into romance is that the people involved don't understand the difference between friendship and intimacy. Too often we confuse the two. With Chelsea, I said I wanted friendship, but I really wanted intimacy. I wanted someone to care about me and love me. My actions betrayed my true desire for the excitement and comfort romance provides.

Were these desires wrong? No, but they were ill-timed. I'm not saying that we should avoid intimacy. We shouldn't. Intimacy is a great thing. But we shouldn't pursue intimacy without commitment. In God-honoring, male-female relationships, the burden of intimacy is commitment in marriage. If we're not ready or capable of committing ourselves to someone, we aren't ready to pursue intimacy.

Remember the analogy we used in chapter 2? Pursuing intimacy without commitment is like going mountain climbing with a partner who, once halfway up the mountain face, isn't sure he or she wants to hold the rope. The last thing you want to hear thousands of feet in the air is that your partner feels tied down in your relationship.

This is exactly what I selfishly did to Chelsea. I wanted the thrill of romance, but I wasn't really ready to make a commitment. Does this mean that I should have married Chelsea since I started the relationship? No, it means that I shouldn't have started an intimate relationship with her in the first place.

Understanding the difference between friendship and intimacy can help us stay within the bounds of friendship until we're ready for the responsibility of an intimate relationship.

2. Be inclusive, not exclusive.

The second step in being just friends with the opposite sex is to include others instead of isolating ourselves with just one person. We don't want dating's mind-set of being alone to carry into our friendships. We can avoid this by going out of our way to involve friends, family, and maybe even strangers in our lives.

Please note that including others doesn't mean finding a token chaperone so you can go on a date. I know more than one couple who brings along a younger brother or sister when they go out so they can call their date a group activity. The local Bible college that many of my friends attend has a rule that students can go out only with a "social unit" of three people. I once had friends invite me to do something with them only to find they had invited me because they needed an extra person to complete a social unit. Thanks, guys! Neither of these examples has the needs of the third party in mind. For all intents and purposes, the younger sibling or the third piece of the social unit might as well be bound and gagged in the trunk!

I'm not talking about inclusion for the sake of appearances. Instead, inclusion must stem from a sincere desire to involve as many people as possible in fellowship and service. So we really shouldn't even start with a couple and try to build from there. We should start with the final goal in mind—such as fellowship, service, prayer, or study of God's Word—then seek to involve others.

When we find ourselves balking at including others, we need to ask ourselves whether friendship is the real motive of our relationship.

3. *Seek opportunities to serve, not to be entertained.*
The late Curt Cobain captured the attitude of today's culture with the line, "Here we are; now entertain us." I believe that, unfortunately, many Christians have made Cobain's line the refrain of their friendships.

In my opinion, our cultural obsession with entertainment is really just an expression of selfishness. The focus in entertainment is not producing something useful for the benefit of others but consuming something for the pleasure of self. And a friendship based on this self-serving, pleasure-seeking mind-set can easily slip into a similarly self-serving romantic relationship that meets the needs of the moment.

But when we shift our relationship orientation from entertainment to service, our friendships move from a focus on ourselves to a focus on the people we can serve. And here's the punch line: In service we find true friendship. In service we can know our friends in a deeper way than ever before.

Stop a moment and give this idea some thought. What can you learn about someone by sitting next to him or her in a movie theater? In contrast, what can you learn about someone while serving side by side with that person? When we break out of the entertainment mind-set and serve others, we not only please God, we receive the blessing of the most fulfilling experience of friendship—two people (or more!), side by side, traveling toward a common, noble purpose.

I'm not saying we can't ever seek entertainment. But I do think we should seek to serve first. So serve soup at a mission before you sit at home and watch a video. Get a group of friends together to teach the fifth-graders at church before you ask the youth pastor to take you to the water-slide park. Start a band in your garage before you go to another concert or buy another CD. Produce before you consume; serve before you seek entertainment.

Maybe someday the anthem of culture will be "Here we are; how can we serve?"

BROTHERLY LOVE

Being just friends with members of the opposite sex doesn't happen by accident. We have to fight for and guard our friendships. Like magnets, men and women are designed to attract each other. But until we're ready to be "stuck for life," we need to avoid premature intimacy. How do we do that? By respecting the limitations of guy-girl friendships and relating to others within the framework given by God's Word. In Romans 12:10-11 we read, "Be devoted to one another in brotherly love. Honor one another above yourselves. Never be lacking in zeal, but keep your spiritual fervor, serving the Lord."

What's our relationship to each other? We're brothers and sisters in Christ.

How do we view treat each other? With honor.

And what's the secret to our zeal? Service—side by side for God's glory.

Guided by this attitude, being "just friends" can be just plain awesome.

CHAPTER TEN

Guard Your Heart

HOW TO FIGHT THE POLLUTANTS OF LUST, INFATUATION, AND SELF-PITY

Emily sprawled lazily on the bed as she watched Jessica pack. "I bet I know what'll happen when you get to school," she said suddenly.

"Oh, really," Jessica replied distractedly. She was more concerned now with how to organize the mess of clothing, shoes, and makeup that covered her bedroom floor.

"Yeah, really," Emily said as she threw a pair of socks at Jessica. She could tell when she wasn't being taken seriously.

"You're going to get there, meet some guy, and fall in love. Then you'll have to crawl back—on your knees—and beg me to forgive you for all the hassle you've given me about dating. Oh, I can't wait until you have a boyfriend!"

If anyone besides Emily had said this, Jessica would have been angry. But coming from her best friend—infuriating though she was—Jessica had to smile.

"Emily, I've told you before that it's not a matter of not wanting to fall in love," Jessica said as she crammed another pair of jeans into her suitcase. "I'm just not interested in playing games and chasing after pointless relationships...like *some* people I know."

Choosing to ignore Jessica's jab, Emily replied, "You just wait; college will change your mind."

WHEN THE RULES DON'T FIT THE GAME

Seven months later, Jessica sat in her room looking out the window at a squirrel hopping across the parking lot. It was one of those rare moments in the afternoon when the dorm was quiet enough for Jessica to think. "Maybe Emily was right," Jessica mused as she replayed the conversation in her mind. College had turned her world topsy-turvy. All of her idealistic views of love and the perfect courtship seemed out-of-date and old-fashioned. She'd arrived at college so sure of things; now she didn't know what she believed.

Growing up in a small town with few Christian guys, Jessica hadn't really considered dating. Her girlfriends provided her plenty of companionship; and homework, volleyball, and softball kept her busy. During her junior year of high school, Jessica heard a speaker at a youth conference give a message called "A Biblical Perspective on Romance." He talked about how dating often contradicted scriptural principles. Jessica was surprised at how much sense the speaker's ideas made. She had never consciously "not dated," but now she understood why she had always felt uncomfortable with the concept. Jessica began mentally cataloging the many times her friends had been hurt by dating relationships that had turned sour. Hadn't she seen how negative dating could be?

Thus Jessica began her search for the "right" way of doing things. Or, as Emily put it, Jessica went "ballistic on her anti-dating campaign." She scoured the Bible for insight, read books, listened to tapes on the subject, and spent more than a few evenings talking—often arguing—with her friends about the merits and pitfalls of dating.

From this quest Jessica emerged with her own "rules of romance," like a modern-day Moses descending from Mount Sinai with the Ten Commandments. She felt sure that her list of do's and don'ts would solve the world's relational problems…or at least keep *her* from experiencing them. First, Jessica wouldn't allow herself to get bogged down in short-term relationships. Until she felt she could pursue marriage, dating was out; she would only go out with guys in groups. At the point when romance was appropriate, a guy who showed interest in her would first have to talk with her parents. From this point, Jessica had every detail of the courtship process planned like a carefully written screenplay. After checking out the prospective suitor, Mom and Dad would give the young man permission to woo her, the two of them would fall hopelessly in love, and the sun would shine at their outdoor wedding.

All this was good. Wisely, Jessica had developed high standards. In fact, her rules were sound. But her method of developing her guidelines lacked something. Jessica had calculated her dating standards with the emotional detachment of Spock. Yes, her rules made sense, but they were just rules—they hadn't come to life in her heart. And only those beliefs springing from the heart can ever hope to stand the rushing winds of emotion. For Jessica, the storm was about to break.

When she arrived at college (a very conservative Christian school chosen in part because of its strict guidelines), Jessica found to her dismay that all the outward rules she had counted on did nothing to control the feelings that suddenly began to well up inside her. She had never interacted with so many handsome, godly guys on a daily basis. Jessica had never had a problem turning down a date with Tony, who wore a Metallica T-shirt and sported stringy bleached hair. But when tall, clean-cut

Eric gazed at her with his penetrating brown eyes as he discussed that morning's chapel sermon, Jessica felt her resolve melting.

To make matters worse, she couldn't look ten feet without seeing a couple. They were everywhere! Three out of her four roommates had boyfriends and looked on her lack of attachment in bewilderment, if not disdain. Jessica felt like a nun on the "Love Boat."

Inside, Jessica began to covet her roommates' relationships. Suddenly the thought of having a boyfriend seemed so comforting. She found herself daydreaming about certain guys. "What if so-and-so is 'the one'? What did he *really* mean when he said such-and-such? Does he like me?" With all these thoughts swimming in her head, Jessica became wistful and discontented. No matter what she did, she'd think, "If only I could share this with someone." She had more than enough girlfriends and several guy friends, but they hardly fulfilled the longing she felt.

To make things even more difficult, guys were beginning to ask her out. Were any of them husband material? Not quite, but one was cute.... Deep down Jessica knew she was doing all the things she had resolved not to, but did it even matter now? Her standards and rules seemed worthless.

GETTING ACQUAINTED

The human heart doesn't like taking orders from the mind. The time will come for all of us when we won't *feel* like doing the godly, responsible thing we've resolved to do. The question is, how will we respond when our hearts lead a full-scale rebellion? If we don't prepare ourselves for an uprising, we'll feel tempted to abandon our principles and standards.

"As I grew into womanhood," writes Elisabeth Elliot in *Passion and Purity*, "and began to learn what was in my heart I saw very clearly that, of all things difficult to rule, none were more so than my will and affections." The sooner we get acquainted with the contents of our hearts, the better. Too many of us are blissfully unaware of how deceitful the core of our beings can truly be. When we think "heart," we picture cutesy, red, cut-out valentines. But often, if we'd really examine our hearts, we'd find lies, selfishness, lust, envy, and pride. And that's the abridged list! The effect is like discovering your sweet old grandmother's picture on the FBI's Most Wanted list at the post office.

But though we might be surprised, God is not. He not only understands the fragility of the human heart, He knows how easily it can be swayed in the wrong direction.

THE DECEITFUL HEART

The Bible is replete with warnings about the nature of the human heart and with instructions to make our top priority watching over it. Proverbs 4:23 tells us, "Above all else, guard your heart..." How should we do this?

First, picture guarding your heart as if your heart were a criminal tied in a chair who would like to break free and knock you over the head. In other words, protect yourself from your heart's sinfulness. Keep a wary eye on your heart, knowing that it can do you damage if it is not carefully watched.

"The heart is deceitful above all things..." we read in Jeremiah 17:9. "Who can know it?" Though the advice of many well-meaning people today is to "follow your heart," the Bible warns that your heart can lead you in wrong, even deadly, directions. Our hearts lie. Something can "feel" right and be completely wrong.

In his book *First Things First,* Stephen Covey uses an analogy that can help us understand the knack our emotions have for bending reality. If you take a flashlight and shine it on a sundial at night, you can make the sundial tell any time you want. But while this method gives you a time, that time won't be accurate. Why? Because you've manipulated the source of light.

In the same way, our emotions can "shed light" on our circumstances from any number of angles. They can tell us whatever we want to hear. But we can't place all our trust in these heart readings.

Julie, a nineteen-year old who worked as a receptionist in a doctor's office, found herself deeply attracted to her boss, a married man who was beginning to make advances toward her. She wanted to act on her attraction and play along with his flirting. Her heart told her to give in to her feelings. Should she have listened?

Fortunately, Julie's convictions resisted the whisperings of her heart. She quit her job and confessed her temptation to a Christian friend who prayed with her and promised to keep her accountable.

Julie wisely guarded her heart by thinking through the consequences of her actions. If she followed her feelings, she would sin against God, she would carry the memory of the affair into her future marriage, and she would possibly ruin the man's marriage and family. Thinking along these lines exposed the ugliness of her heart's desires. Getting away from the temptation and finding an accountability partner were further precautions to ensure that she didn't fall prey to her own sinful heart.

Do you face a potentially precarious situation that your heart wants you to pursue? Like Julie, do whatever it takes to guard your heart and keep it in submission to God.

MAINTAINING A PURE SPRING

Next, picture guarding your heart as if it were a fresh spring of water that you want to drink from daily. The Bible tells us the heart is "the wellspring of life" (Proverbs 4:23), the source of our attitudes, words, and deeds. If we fail to keep our hearts clean, the rest of our lives will stagnate and become dirty.

Peter Marshall, the former chaplain of the United States Senate, loved to tell a story called "The Keeper of the Spring." This simple tale beautifully illustrates the importance of constantly maintaining the purity of our hearts.

An elderly, quiet forest dweller once lived high above an Austrian village along the eastern slopes of the Alps. Many years ago, the town council had hired this old gentleman as Keeper of the Spring to maintain the purity of the pools of water in the mountain crevices. The overflow from these pools ran down the mountainside and fed the lovely spring which flowed through the town. With faithful, silent regularity, the Keeper of the Spring patrolled the hills, removed the leaves and branches from the pools, and wiped away the silt that would otherwise choke and contaminate the fresh flow of water. By and by, the village became a popular attraction for vacationers. Graceful swans floated along the crystal-clear spring, the mill wheels of various businesses located near the water turned day and night, farmlands were naturally irrigated, and the view from restaurants sparkled.

Years passed. One evening the town council met for its semiannual meeting. As the council members reviewed the budget, one man's eye caught the salary paid the obscure Keeper of the Spring. "Who is this old man?" he asked indignantly. "Why do we keep paying him year after year? No one ever sees him. For all we know, this man does us no good. He isn't necessary any longer!" By a unanimous vote, the council dispensed with the old man's services.

For several weeks nothing changed. But by early autumn, the trees began to shed their leaves. Small branches snapped off and fell into the pools, hindering the rushing flow of sparkling water. One afternoon, someone noticed a slight yellowish-brown tint in the spring. A few days later, the water had darkened even more. Within a week, a slimy film covered sections of the water along the banks, and a foul odor emanated from the spring. The mill wheels moved slowly; some finally ground to a halt. Businesses located near the water closed. The swans migrated to fresher waters far away, and tourists no longer visited the town. Eventually, the clammy fingers of disease and sickness reached deeply into the village.

The shortsighted town council enjoyed the beauty of the spring but underestimated the importance of guarding its source. We can make the same mistake in our lives. Like the Keeper of the Spring who maintained the purity of the water, you and I are the Keepers of Our Hearts. We need to consistently evaluate the purity of our hearts in prayer, asking God to reveal the little things that contaminate us. As God reveals our wrong attitudes, longings, and desires, we must remove them from our hearts.

POLLUTANTS

What are some things God will ask us to remove from our hearts, especially concerning our dating mentality? "Do not love the world," John warns us, "or anything in the world...For everything in the world—the cravings of sinful man, the lust of his eyes, and the boasting of what he has and does—comes not from the Father, but from the world" (1 John 2:15–16). In this passage, John gives us three categories of worldly things that pollute our hearts: sinful cravings, lust, and prideful comparison with others. Can we apply these items to romantic relationships? I think so. In fact, most of our struggles in relationships seem to involve desiring what we shouldn't desire, lusting after what God has forbidden, or complaining about what we don't have. These "pollutants" specifically manifest themselves in relationships as infatuation, lust, and self-pity. Let's examine all three more closely.

1. Infatuation

You've probably experienced it—the constant thoughts about someone who has caught your eye, the heart palpitations whenever that person walks by, the hours spent dreaming of a future with that special someone. It's infatuation, and I know it well, having experienced it myself!

Many of us have a difficult time seeing infatuation as potentially harmful. But we need to examine it carefully, because when you really think about it, infatuation can be a sinful response to attraction. Any time we allow someone to displace God as the focus of our affection, we've moved from innocent appreciation of someone's beauty or personality to the dangerous realm of infatuation. Instead of making God the object of our longing, we wrongly direct these feelings toward another human. We become idolaters, bowing to someone other than God, hoping that this person will meet our needs and bring fulfillment.

God is righteously jealous for our hearts; after all, he has created us and redeemed us. He wants us to focus our thoughts, longings, and desires on him. He lovingly blesses us with human relationships, but he first calls us to find our heart's delight in him.

In addition to diverting our attention from God, infatuation can cause problems for us because it is most often founded on illusion. When infatuated with someone, we tend to build up that person in our imaginations as the perfect guy or girl. We think we'd be happy forever if that person would return our affections. Of course, we can only sustain our silly crush because we've substituted fantasy for all the information we lack about the person. As soon as we get to know that person's true identity and discover that our "perfect" man or woman is human like everyone else, our dreams fade and we move on to a new crush.

To break out of this pattern of infatuation, we must reject the notion that a human relationship can ever completely fulfill us. When we find our hearts slipping into the fantasy world of infatuation, we should pray, "Lord, help me to appreciate this person without elevating him (or her) above You in my heart. Help me to remember that no human can ever take Your place in my life. You are my strength, my hope, my joy, and my ultimate reward. Bring me back to reality, God; 'give me an undivided heart'" (Psalm 86:11).

My dad likes to say that when you let God be God you can let humans be human. When we place God in His rightful place in our lives, we don't struggle so much when human relationships let us down. In direct contrast, when we make another human our idol, God can't be our God.

After placing God first in our lives, we need to continue to avoid infatuation by resolving to *not* feed attraction. "Don't nurse a crush!" a girl from Brooklyn, New York, told me when I asked her how she beats infatuation. And she's right. Attraction only grows into infatuation when we pamper it.

Each time we find ourselves attracted to someone, we have a choice to either leave it at attraction or allow our imaginations to carry us away. I was once a guest on a radio talk show, and afterward I talked to the producer, a single woman in her thirties. She told me teenagers aren't the only ones who deal with crushes. This beautiful, intelligent woman still had to resist infatuation as an adult. She made a statement that I have found very helpful. "Joshua," she said after telling me the story of a gentleman who had recently been pursuing her, "I want to stay focused on God. Until the right man comes along, I refuse to feed romantic expectations and let my heart get carried away." For her, feeding romantic expectations meant daydreaming about a guy on the way home from work, putting his picture on the refrigerator, and giggling about him with friends. At the right time in a relationship, each of these activities might be appropriate, but before the proper time, she knew these actions would only lead to fantasy-based infatuation.

How about you? Have you found yourself succumbing to infatuation, removing your focus from God, and fantasizing about the "perfect" partner? Perhaps you need to take a step back and evaluate the role infatuation plays in your life.

2. Lust

The second poison that often threatens the purity of our hearts is lust. To lust is to crave something sexually that God has forbidden. For example, when I as a single man look on a woman who is not my wife (which right now means every woman) and immorally fantasize about her, I am lusting; I am setting my heart on something God has placed off limits. Sexual desire within marriage is a natural and appropriate expression of sexuality; after all, God gave us our sex drives. But God also gives us specific commands forbidding us to indulge in those desires before we marry.

To fight lust in our lives, we have to detest it with the same intensity God does. Unfortunately, we often do not. An experience I had while visiting Denver, Colorado, opened my eyes to my own laxity toward lust. One afternoon I was walking from my hotel to the convention center downtown. A group of three guys walked past me in the opposite direction. They smiled in a way that seemed odd. They whispered and laughed as they passed me, and for some reason, those actions made me uncomfortable. What was bothering me? I pushed my discomfort out of my mind and went on. But a few moments later a car pulled up alongside me. The same three guys were inside. This time, I could in no way mistake their intent nor the reason I'd felt strange—these guys were homosexuals and were checking me out. They whistled, winked, and laughed at my bafflement. Finally they sped away, leaving me to fume.

I'll never forget the anger and disgust I felt at that moment. I was outraged to have served as the object of their lust, to have their eyes crawling over me. It was so wrong, so filthy.

I remember turning to God in self-righteous anger and hissing through my clenched teeth, "Those people are so sick!"

The gentle rebuke God whispered to *my* heart caught me off guard.

"Joshua, your smug heterosexual lust is just as misplaced, just as disgusting in My sight."

This realization floored me. My contempt at the lust of those three men was *nothing* in comparison to the disgust God feels at the lust in *my* heart, even though society condones and expects it. God states that when I look at a woman lustfully, whether she is on the street, on a billboard, or in a movie, I'm actually committing adultery with her in my heart (Matthew 5:28). That's serious!

How many times have I felt lust for a passing girl as those homosexual men felt for me? How many times have my eyes slid across a woman's body like a "slug on a rose" as Cyrano de Bergerac so aptly described it? Am I as repulsed by lust in *my* life as I am by lust in others'? Beilby Porteus writes, "What we are afraid to do before men, we should be afraid to think before God."

We should seek to completely remove lust from our minds. We should pray, "'Create in me a pure heart, O God' (Psalm 51:10). Help me to be like Job, who made a covenant with his eyes not to look lustfully at others (Job 31:1). Forgive me for pampering lust in my life; help me to guard against it faithfully. May the 'meditations of my heart be pleasing in your sight, O LORD'" (Psalm 19:14).

Finally, we need to avoid those things that encourage wrong desire. For one girl I know, guarding her heart against lust meant throwing away all her secular romance novels. She felt convicted that the constant sensuality those books featured was totally inappropriate for her to read, making her heart rich soil for seeds of lust. Another friend attending college stopped spending his afternoons at the beach because the bikini-clad girls there were too great a temptation for his eyes. Another male friend decided to abstain from all movies for six months. All three of these friends are examples of people, each with different weaknesses, guarding their hearts from those things— books, locations, movies—that lead to sinful desires.

When we evaluate our lives honestly enough to recognize our own lust and see the sorrow it causes God, we'll want to destroy lust…before it destroys us.

3. *Self-Pity*

The final pollutant of our hearts is self-pity. In a sense, self-pity is the worship of our circumstances. When we indulge in feeling sorry for ourselves, we turn our focus from God—His goodness, His justice, His ability to save in any circumstance. And as we turn away from God, we cut ourselves off from our only source of hope.

We can so easily allow self-pity to seep into our hearts. When we feel lonely or crave someone to love and be loved by, it seems we have every reason in the world to complain, to sulk angrily because we've received a bum deal.

But do we really have reason to complain when we consider the Cross? As I try to follow God's plan for relationships and, as a result, pass up short-term dating, I'm sometimes tempted to fall into a "martyr" mentality. "Oh, woe is me! Here I am, suffering for righteousness!" What foolishness! In my more objective moments, I imagine God's response to my self-pity as similar to the message of a popular T-shirt: "Would you like some cheese with your whine?" Spending my time sighing over what I've given up doesn't impress God; obeying Him with joy does.

Self-pity is a sinful response to feelings of loneliness. We don't sin when we feel lonely or admit a desire for companionship, but we do sin when we use these feelings as an excuse to turn from God and exalt our own needs.

Do you often find yourself focusing on your own sorry state and not relying on God to do His best for you? If so, then you probably need to take an honest look at your tendency toward self-pity. If you need to, you can defuse self-pity by doing several things. First, stop basing your happiness on how you compare with other people. Don't get sucked into the comparison game. Too many people waste their lives pursuing things they don't really want just because they can't bear the idea of someone having something they don't. Ask yourself this question: "Am I really lacking something in my life, or am I just coveting what someone else has?"

Next, when you feel those old feelings of self-pity rising,

redirect them into compassion for others. Look around for someone who might share your feelings of loneliness, and find a way to comfort that person. Get your focus off your needs, and help meet someone else's.

Finally, learn to use feelings of loneliness as an opportunity to draw closer to God. A girl in her midtwenties who recently married told me that she saw loneliness as God's call to her heart. "When I felt lonely, I would think, 'God is calling me back to Him,'" she told me. During these times she learned to pour out her heart to God and talk with Him. Now she wouldn't trade those intimate moments with God for the world.

HE KNOWS ALL THINGS

The job of guarding our hearts is a big responsibility. It takes place in the secret places of devotion. In honest prayer and meditation on God's Word, we scrape the film of infatuation, lust, and self-pity from our hearts. And as with the Keeper of the Spring, the work is never done. We must police our hearts with "faithful, silent regularity."

Yes, our hearts are deceitful, but the promise of 1 John 3:20 gives us hope in our labor: "For God is greater than our hearts, and he knows everything." God's strength can help see us through the upheavals of our emotions. And we can take comfort in the knowledge that He doesn't view our plight from a distance, shaking His head at our weakness. Jesus, the Son of God who Hebrews 7:25 tells us "always lives to intercede" for us, has endured the same feelings of loneliness you and I have, and He understands how it feels to face temptation. He will help and sustain us as we trust in Him and faithfully guard our hearts.

CHAPTER ELEVEN

"You Don't Date? What Are You, Nuts?"

WHAT TO DO WHEN PEOPLE ASK
WHY YOU DON'T PLAY THE DATING GAME

One day, my seven-year-old brother, Brett, informed me matter-of-factly that Susie from Sunday school had a crush on him.

"Is that right?" I said.

"Uh-huh," Brett said nonchalantly. "She named her teddy bear Brett, and she kisses it in church."

"She does what?"

"And she kissed me, too. She wants me to be her boyfriend."

"She what?"

Needless to say, there was a small eruption at the Harris home. My parents informed Brett that he didn't need to worry about having a girlfriend and that he shouldn't let girls kiss him.

This incident humorously illustrates something that's not always funny: pressure from others to pair up. You've probably felt it in one form or another. Whether from friends, family, or even strangers, we all face the push to conform to our culture's expectations for relationships. Most people around us expect us to date; when we don't, they often challenge our standards, sometimes mock us, and always ask a lot of questions. How should we respond?

In this chapter, I'd like to give you ideas for confidently communicating your decision to, at present, avoid dating. To do this, I'll give a few examples of situations you'll most likely face and some principles that can guide you through these predicaments.

SCENE ONE: CONFRONTATION IN THE SCHOOL CAFETERIA

Sean Missler sat in the school cafeteria, finishing his lunch of stiff French fries and a soft drink. As the other students cleared out, Randy Johnson walked up and greeted Sean with his typical self-assured smile.

"What's up, bro?" Randy asked as he sidled up to Sean's table.

"Not much. You want some fries?"

"Uh, no thanks," Randy said, after glancing at the cold potato sticks. "Listen, I wanted to find out who you're taking to the banquet. I'm going with Jenny, and I was thinking you and your date could come over to my house afterward. My mom said we could use the hot tub. Oh, my gosh, have you seen Jenny in a bathing suit? Yow! So, whadda ya say?"

"Well, I don't know, Randy, I don't think..."

"C'mon, man! What about Melissa Summers? Now she is fine!"

"No, I don't really..."

"What are you talking about? Of course you want to!" Randy said as he playfully punched Sean's arm.

"Look, Randy, I'm not going to the banquet, okay?"

"Not going?"

"Well, yeah. Andrew, Ben, and I were planning on taking my sister and a few girls from church to dinner then going to my house to play games and stuff."

"Games?"

"Yeah, you know, Scrabble and stuff like that."

"Scrabble? I could set you up with Melissa, and you want to go out to dinner with your sister and a bunch of dateless losers and then play Scrabble? Buddy, you've lost your mind!"

"They are not losers! We just want to go out as friends. You go out with Jenny, but don't give me a hard time if I don't want to join you."

"Hey, I'm not down on your friends. But look, Sean, when was the last time you went out with someone—I mean, really went out with a girl? Man, now's the time to get the action going."

"Yeah, thanks for the advice," Sean said caustically as Randy stood up to leave.

When Randy reached the cafeteria door, he turned and called back, "Hey, Missler! I've got a great five-across word for your Scrabble game: F-R-E-A-K!"

"Very funny," Sean said under his breath as his friend's laughter faded down the hall.

HUMBLE, NOT SNAPPY, ANSWERS

If you've ever faced a similar situation, then you know how aggravating it can be. But though it's not always easy, we have to learn to stand by our convictions without becoming bitter toward those who disagree with us or make fun of us. When we communicate our views to others, we need to watch ourselves so we don't come across as cynical, sarcastic, or defensive.

Mad magazine, known for its outrageous humor and general craziness, used to have a regular cartoon called "Snappy Answers to Stupid Questions." The underlying premise of the cartoon was if someone asks a dumb question, he or she deserves an equally dumb answer. For example, one cartoon showed a person asking a girl who has a phone to her ear, "Are you on the phone?" The girl on the phone sarcastically responds, "No, this is a giant Q-tip."

I mention this because this attitude is the exact opposite of the one we want to have as people question our decision not to date. We don't want to give "Snappy Answers to Stupid Questions" but rather humble, Christ-honoring answers to any question, even if it sounds stupid to us. We don't want to put people off when we express our beliefs; we want to submit to our own convictions and communicate them lovingly so people can hear them. So our first principle of communication is this:

We should communicate our convictions about dating with humility and from a desire to please God, not to put others down.

When we approach something differently from others, we can so easily fall into a defensive, critical mind-set. Some people I know (including myself, I'm afraid) have expressed our standards for dating smugly and self-righteously. These attitudes are completely wrong. We communicate and live by our convictions in order to please God and serve those around us, not in order to feel superior or to look down on others. God hates pride and self-righteousness, and we should avoid those attitudes whenever we discuss our standards.

SCENE TWO: AUNT TESSI

"Orange, avocado, and gold," Sarah thought to herself. "Everything in my aunt's house is orange, avocado, or gold," she mused as she sipped ice tea from an old Care Bear collectors glass and stood in her Aunt Tessi's living room.

Just then her mother and Tessi entered from the kitchen. Tessi gave Sarah a hug. "Mmm, you smell good, Sarah-Barah," she said. "Where'd you get that pretty perfume?" And then, raising her eyebrow, "A boy?"

"Well, yeah," Sarah said mischievously as she plopped on the floor next to the coffee table.

Sarah's mom smiled as she made herself cozy on the couch.

"Who?" Tessi practically screamed. "Who is it? Are you keeping secrets from me? Who?"

"Dad!" Sarah said triumphantly.

"Ooh, you're such a tease," Tessi said as she joined Sarah's mom on the couch. "But now really, tell me all about your love life."

"Here we go again," Sarah thought as she ran her fingers through the gold shag carpet. Every time she saw her aunt, Sarah had to face the same barrage of questions about her single status. Aunt Tessi didn't grasp the concept of not dating.

"Oh, Tess, don't get started with that again," Sarah's mother said, coming to her rescue. "Sarah is only sixteen, and I've told you before that Robert and I don't want her to date. Kids get into so much trouble these days. Besides, Sarah's involved at church, and she wants to go to college. There's no point in getting distracted."

"She needs a boyfriend!" Tessi sang out as if she hadn't heard a word her sister had said. "She's such a beautiful girl; she shouldn't be deprived. Did I tell you that Angie is seeing the nicest boy from Clark College? They met at one of the sorority parties. He's studying to be a…" When Aunt Tessi got rolling, there was no point in trying to stop her. She would go on about Sarah's cousin's latest boyfriend for another half-hour before taking her next breath.

Sarah looked at her mom, who sighed and smiled at Sarah.

Sarah's mom was used to Aunt Tessi too. The look in her eyes communicated support: "Don't worry, girl. You're on the right track; don't let this discourage you."

VINDICATION IS OVERRATED

When you decide to put off dating, you'll no doubt encounter someone like Aunt Tessi (if you're not already related to one) who doesn't care about logic, values, or biblical principles. You can argue and debate with this type of person until you're blue in the face, but he or she will still think you should immediately hop on the dating bandwagon.

When you interact with people like this, remember the following principle:

You don't have to prove someone wrong
to do what you know is right.

Don't concern yourself with being right in others' eyes. And don't secretly hope that their lives will fall apart so that your opinion will be vindicated. Instead, concentrate on obeying God in your own life and, when possible, helping others to obey Him as well. You don't have to prove others wrong to continue on the course you know God has shown you.

Sometimes after I share my convictions, people still strongly disagree with me. They see things differently. And that's fine. If those people continue in relationships I think are unwise, I pray that God will show them the same mercy He has shown me. But I don't continue to hound them; God will work in their lives when they're ready.

Often the most convincing argument is simply the example

of your own life. We need to respect people's prerogative to disagree with us and hope that our own example will in some way draw them closer to obedience to God.

Scene Three: Sunday Afternoon Dilemma

The Taylor family prided itself on being the last to leave the church each Sunday. Their oldest son, Paul, had long since given up trying to hurry his mom and dad. So as his parents talked happily with another couple, Paul excused himself and wandered into the church parking lot, where he spotted a cluster of his friends standing by their cars.

"Hey, Paul!" a female voice called out. It was Alisha Johnson.

Alisha was new at Preston Valley Bible Church, but she had quickly gotten to know the kids in the youth group. She was outgoing, energetic, and in the words of more than one guy at Preston Valley, "drop-dead gorgeous."

"How are you, Alisha?" Paul asked as he approached the group. "What's the gang doing this afternoon?"

"Paul!" one of the guys in the group called out. "We're going to Wall Street Pizza for lunch and then heading down to the river. Wanna come?"

"Oh, do." Alisha said as she grabbed his arm.

Something about the way Alisha plaintively said "do" made Paul's heart beat faster.

She leaned closer to him and began straightening his tie. "Mr. Taylor," she said in mock seriousness, "you need to come to the river."

"Yeah?" he said, trying not to seem flustered by her attention.

"Yes! Listen, I've got my car here. You can ride to my house and wait for me while I change; then we can meet up with everyone else for pizza. Afterward, I can give you a ride home from the river."

He wanted to say yes—any guy in the world would say yes to Alisha Johnson—but Paul knew it just wasn't right. Alisha's voice and actions were not-so-subtle hints that Alisha was interested in him as more than a brother in Christ. Alisha knew he didn't date, and she wasn't exactly proposing a date, but agreeing to her proposal would be moving in the wrong direction. Paul didn't want to get into a romantic relationship.

Paul pictured the two of them alone at her house—Alisha's mom was single and worked on weekends. Not good. The two of them would arrive together at the restaurant. The rest of the group would start viewing them as a couple. Then Alisha would drive him home that night. Alisha was fun and beautiful, but Paul knew he needed to stay focused for now. Going with her would send a mixed message. He couldn't play games with her heart.

"You know I'd really love to go," he said smiling sadly, "but my parents like me to stick close to home on Sundays. We have some friends coming over this afternoon, so I'm afraid I'll have to pass."

"Well, okay," Alisha said with a small pout as she turned back to the group. "I'll see you on Wednesday then."

"Sounds good," Paul said. "Hey, guys, have a good time today," he yelled as he walked back toward the church building.

His parents were just finishing their conversation.

RUNNING OUT OF EXCUSES

Paul faced a tough dilemma. Enduring the scorn of friends and the derision of relatives is one thing, but having to turn down dates gets old fast. How can you do it without coming across as a hermit? One girl e-mailed me, "Help! I've turned down two dates in the last week. I'm running out of excuses!"

For this girl and for Paul, a time will come when excuses won't suffice. They'll have to explain why they don't currently want to pursue a relationship.

This leads us to the third principle of communicating our beliefs about dating:

> *Our primary purpose for communicating with others should be their encouragement and growth.*

This principle means that sometimes we should explain our convictions and reasons for not dating in detail and other times we shouldn't. Sometimes our explanations are helpful, protecting others' feelings and possibly even challenging them. But other times our rationale only confuses people, ruining a chance for the natural growth of friendship and sending out a holier-than-thou signal.

So how do we decide when to share our views with others? It's not an easy call, but we can learn to differentiate between the good and bad times by understanding the two types of relationships in our lives: those that are merely limited acquaintances and those that are established and ongoing.

When I don't feel close to a person, I rarely dive into a discussion about my views on dating. People who don't know me well might misinterpret my statements or think I am being judgmental. So, for example, if a person who is new at church asks me if I'm seeing someone, I smile nicely and say that I'm not in a relationship at the moment. Launching into a discussion of the seven habits of highly defective dating would be overkill.

On the other hand, I do explain my convictions to my close friends. They know I don't want to be "set up" with anyone and that I want only friendships until I'm ready for marriage. I've discussed this with my friends and shared books and articles that have influenced my thinking. Whether or not my friends agree, I've invested the time to explain where I stand. This makes my life much easier and protects their feelings. For example, I once made plans to go to a movie with a group of friends. At the last minute, everyone backed out except for one girl. But because she knew I avoided one-on-one dates with girls, she called to say we'd need to reschedule. Her feelings weren't hurt, and I didn't have to go into a major explanation. She respected and worked with my beliefs.

When the time comes to share why you don't date, what should you say? Whatever words you use, remember that the goal of your communication is not winning a debate or convincing your hearers of your view. If your friends agree, great! But your main goal is to humbly communicate what you feel God has shown you, to encourage your friends, and to contribute to their growth.

As you explain your stance on dating, make specific statements about your own life, not general statements about everyone else. Remember, it's not your responsibility to live everyone else's life for them, just your own. Focus on what God has spoken to your heart. Be humble and honest about how you're trying to be obedient. If you maintain this humble spirit, you'll often find your listener willing to share his or her own struggles and questions. This opens up the opportunity for you to give counsel and support.

REVILED, WE BLESS

Our key motive in communicating our beliefs about dating should be to serve others. We want to promote peace, love, and righteousness that will bring glory to God. When we feel overly concerned about people's opinions of us, when we concentrate on proving we're "right," we're likely to become defensive and overbearing. But when we make our top priority showing God's love to others and thinking of their feelings, we'll find it easier to make wise decisions about what we do and do not say.

When you get one of those "You don't date? Are you nuts?" looks from people, adopt the apostle Paul's attitude when he described the abuse we suffer for following Christ: "Being reviled, we bless; being persecuted, we endure it; being defamed, we entreat" (1 Corinthians 4:12–13, NKJV).

The Bible tells us we're to bear the pain of ridicule without flinching. Have you faced scorn from people who don't understand your convictions about dating? Instead of lashing out, respond with kindness, and ask God to show those people the same mercy He has shown you.

PART FOUR

Now What?

CHAPTER TWELVE

Redeeming the Time

MAKING THE MOST OF YOUR SINGLENESS

"Look at this," my mom said, handing me a card. "We're invited to a reception for Jenny and her new husband."

I stared at the invitation and the couple pictured on it. My jaw dropped. "I can't believe this," I said. "Jenny Renquist is married? This is impossible!"

"What do you mean, it's impossible?" Mom asked.

"I liked her in eighth grade!" I said. "How can she be married?"

"She met a nice guy, and they got married. It happens all the time."

"Why is it happening to all the girls I used to like?" I whined.

"You haven't talked to or thought about Jenny for years," my mother reprimanded. "Don't get wistful all of a sudden."

"I'm not..." I said looking at the picture again. "Mom..."

"Yes?"

"I think my biological clock is ticking."

"Boys don't have biological clocks."

"They don't?"

"No."

"Oh."

MARRIAGE ON THE BRAIN

Whether or not you have a biological clock, and whether or not it's ticking, marriage will inevitably sneak up on you. Your friends' wedding invitations will begin arriving by the dozens. Suddenly, what once seemed far off and unimaginable has become very real. At this point in your life, people who find out you're unattached often develop that matchmaking gleam in their eyes. If you've reached this stage, then you know what I mean. All of those around you mentally pair you up with every available member of the opposite sex they know.

Being of "marriageable age" and single is a precarious condition. Even if marriage isn't at the forefront of your mind, it's guaranteed to be on the minds of those around you. My family proved this to me when I turned twenty-one. In my family, we have a tradition of writing letters to each other on our birthdays. The letters I received on my twenty-first birthday really caught me off guard. Why? Because of the consistent references to the "special someone" who evidently, in the opinion of my parents and younger brother, would pop up any day.

My mom started the trend with this sentence: "I know it will be hard to let you go when you meet that one we're all waiting and praying for."

"The one we're all waiting and praying for"? I thought. Good grief, Mom! I brushed off her comment as a lapse into I.W.G.S. (I Want Grandchildren Syndrome).

Amused, I put down my mom's letter and started reading my dad's. His was full of fatherly advice, but the closing lines picked up the marital theme: "Finally, expect to meet her someday soon, if you haven't met her already. She will be prepared for you by God because 'a good wife is from the Lord.' When you know you have found her, be patient—you needn't rush.

But neither should you need to delay things. Marry her within the year and count on God to help you take care of her."

I swallowed hard when I read those words. I put down the letter, then picked it up and read the lines again. "Expect to meet her soon"? Wow! My dad had never discussed marriage in such serious terms. It seemed so heavy, so grown up.

Then I opened the letter from my twelve-year-old brother and roommate, Joel. He had designed it on the computer and printed it out on my dad's color printer. "Surely," I thought, "Joel couldn't have indulged in this marriage silliness." I was wrong. The end of his note read, "I really treasure sharing a room with you, knowing that someday soon you'll be sharing a room with someone else."

I burst out laughing. My mom was waiting and praying, my dad was expecting me to meet her soon, and my brother was already discussing the wedding night! Nobody had mentioned marriage when I turned eighteen, nineteen, or twenty. But now it was the talk of the town! If I hadn't known better, I might have thought my family had met in a back room and plotted to get me out of the way by marrying me off as quickly as possible.

WHAT DO I DO NOW?

While my family didn't want to push me into matrimony prematurely, their letters did remind me that I had entered a new season of life. At this point in my life, marriage is no longer impossible. If God brought the right person into my life I could, theoretically, do something about it.

While this realization is exhilarating, it's also a little confusing. God *hasn't* brought the right person into my life. My friends who have met and want to marry Mr. or Miss Right may face obstacles such as getting their finances lined up and figuring out housing, but at least they know what they have to do. They've mapped out a course. But my path isn't so clear.

If you've reached the same stage, maybe you're asking the same questions I'm asking: Does the fact that I *could* get married mean I should make it a priority to find someone? Do I assume I'll get married soon or act as if I never will? What am I supposed to do *now*?

Hustle While You Wait

Fortunately, we have a source to turn to when these questions arise. I've found some guidance in the book of Ephesians. Paul writes, "Be very careful, then, how you live—not as unwise but as wise, making the most of every opportunity, because the days are evil" (Ephesians 5:15). Another version reads, "See then that you walk circumspectly, not as fools but as wise, redeeming the time..." (Ephesians 5:15, NKJV).

My mom uses the phrase "hustle while you wait" to express the same idea. If one of us children stands around, picking at food while she cooks dinner, Mom will snap, like a football coach to his players, "Don't just stand there! Hustle while you wait!" That means set the table, put away groceries, or load the dishwasher; be productive during a lull in the action.

My mom has an intolerance for wasted time. I think God has the same intolerance. He has entrusted us with gifts and talents, and He expects us to guard and use them wisely. Will we give Him a return on His investment in us? Even though we don't know the next step regarding our romantic relationships, we still have work to do. We have bad habits to get rid of, good habits to develop, and character to build. Let's hustle!

Yes, we'll still have a lot of questions—we may not know who or when we'll marry. But we must not allow what we *can't know* to hinder us from acting on what we *do know*. And what do we know? We know that we have *today* to move with resolute energy toward maturity and Christlikeness, a calling of every Christian whether he or she will marry next week or ten years from now.

When we focus on "redeeming the time," we'll not only make the most of each moment, we'll also prepare ourselves for the next season of our lives. Our faithfulness in small things today earns us the right to handle bigger responsibilities down the road.

WATERING CAMELS

In the Old Testament, Rebekah is a young woman who "redeemed the time" by faithfully fulfilling her current obligations. We could learn a few things from revisiting the story of how she prepared for, met, and married her husband. The story begins when Abraham sends his oldest and most trusted servant to his hometown to find a wife for his son Isaac. Catherine Vos continues the story this way:

> At last, after several days of travel, he reached the place where Abraham's brother Nahor now lived. This city was called Haran. Outside the city was a well of water. In that dry country there was often only one well for a whole city. Every night the young girls of the city went out to the well, with tall pitchers balanced on their heads. They let down their pitchers into the well and drew water. Then they carried it home on their heads for the family to use.
>
> When Abraham's servant came to Haran, he made his camels kneel down by the well. It was evening—just the

time when the young girls always gathered around the well to draw water.

Abraham's servant believed in God. He had come safely on his journey and had reached the city to which Abraham had sent him. But he thought to himself, "How shall I be able to tell which young girl is the one God wants Isaac to have for his wife?" He kneeled down on the ground beside the well and bowed his head. He prayed, "O LORD God of my master Abraham, help me this day! When the daughters of the people of the city come down to draw water, and I say to one of them, 'Let down your pitcher, I pray you, that I may drink,' and she shall say, 'Drink, and I will give your camels drink also,' let that be the one whom Thou hast appointed as a wife for Isaac."

God often answers prayer almost before we have asked, and He did so this time. Before the servant had finished praying, a very beautiful girl named Rebekah came to the well. The servant thought, "Can this be the right one?" He ran to her and said, "Let me, I pray you, drink a little water out of your pitcher."

The girl said very politely, "Drink, my lord, and I will draw water for your camels also, till they have finished drinking." She took the pitcher down from her head and let him drink. Then she emptied the rest of the water into the drinking trough for the camels. She kept drawing water till all the camels had had a drink.

The servant was very much astonished to have her say and do just as he had prayed that she might. Had his prayer been answered so soon? When the camels had had enough water, he gave Rebekah a rich, gold ring which he had brought with him, and he put on her arms two beautiful gold bracelets.

Then he asked her, "Whose daughter are you? Is
there room in your father's house for us to stay?"

She answered, "I am Nahor's granddaughter. We have
plenty of room for you to stay with us, and straw and
food for your camels." Nahor was Abraham's brother.
When the servant heard this, he was so happy that he
bowed his head down to the ground and worshiped,
saying, "Blessed be the LORD God of my master Abraham,
who has led me to the house of my master's family."

The rest of the story (which you can read in Genesis 24)
tells how Rebekah agreed within two days to return with
Abraham's servant to marry Isaac, a man she had never met.
The tale is, without question, amazing. In their own day, these
events were astonishing; today, separated by thousands of years
and very different cultures, we find them even more astound-
ing. And yet, as with all of God's Word, we can learn a lesson
from this story that transcends time and culture.

Although we don't study the story as a model of how every
couple should meet and marry, we can learn from Rebekah's
attitude and actions. In an article entitled "The Adventure of
Current Obligations" Gregg Harris points out the key principle
of the story: "Rebekah was able to meet God's divine appoint-
ment for her life because she was faithfully carrying out her
current obligations."

For Rebekah, the trip to the well that particular evening was
nothing special. She made that trip every night. And she'd
probably watered more than a few camels. Yet though her task
was mundane, she had a quickness to her step and a ready willingness to serve others. These qualities put her in the right
place at the right time with the right attitude when God intended
to match her with Isaac.

We all have our own camels to water—current relationships and responsibilities we can too easily take for granted. If we're wise, we'll see our duties not as unimportant ways to bide our time, but as springboards, launching us into God's plan and purpose for our future.

PRACTICE NOW

For a moment, take stock of your current attitude. Are you so caught up in dreaming of marriage that you're neglecting your present responsibilities as a son, daughter, brother, sister, or friend? Or are you redeeming the time, fulfilling those responsibilities God has given you today?

We cannot ignore our current responsibilities and expect to magically gain the strength of character and virtue that will make us good husbands and wives. If we aren't faithful and growing in the relationships we have now, we won't be prepared to pursue faithfulness and growth in marriage later.

Someday I want to be a godly husband. I want to nurture my wife, love her, respect her, and protect her. How can I train for that? I believe God has given me a mother and sister to practice understanding and honoring women. If I can't love and serve my mother and sister today, what makes me think I'll be ready to love and serve a wife in the future? I have to practice now. The reverse is true for girls and their dads and brothers. Girls can view their relationships to the men in their lives as training sessions for loving and respecting a future husband.

Marriage won't transform us into new people; it will only act as a mirror, showing what we already are. We have to practice now what we want to be in the future. Let's look at a few areas we can prepare for while we're still single:

Practice intimacy. While we want to avoid premature intimacy in romantic relationships, we should practice intimacy in other committed relationships starting with our families. God has given us families to learn the art of sharing life.

A close female friend of mine realized she had developed bad communication habits with her parents. Whenever they'd try to talk to her, she would clam up and refuse to share her feelings. "It finally hit me," she told me. "If I shut out the people closest to me now, I'll do the same thing someday to my husband." To reverse this trend, my friend now works hard to build intimacy and openness with her folks. Instead of retreating to her bedroom after dinner, she hangs around and talks with them. Instead of shutting them out of her life, she invites them in. This process, which wasn't easy at first, not only strengthens important relationships currently, it teaches her skills she'll need one day as a wife.

Practice seeking God with others. A newlywed friend told me that before he got married, he was used to having uninterrupted time in the morning to pray and write in his journal. Now he had to make room for prayer and devotions with his wife as well as both their private times with God. "I never knew how confusing it could be to coordinate two spiritual lives!" he said.

Each of us must develop a dynamic, growing, personal relationship with God. This involves practicing the spiritual disciplines of prayer, meditation, Bible study, Bible teaching, and involvement in a local church. But in preparation for marriage, we also need to learn to seek God with another person. Again, we don't want to practice this discipline with a romantic interest until we're ready to pursue committed intimacy. But we can develop this habit with other important people in our lives. You might start this process with your family then branch out to pray and study the Bible with safe, nonromantic friends from church. Learn to share with others the lessons God teaches you. Learn to pray with someone else. Be honest about your areas of weakness, and ask God for a trusted person to keep you accountable to growing in the Lord.

Recently I was with a group of four friends—one guy and three girls. We had spent the day hiking then had returned to my house to relax and talk. One of the girls began to talk about how God had dealt with her on different issues of obedience. Her testimony led to a spontaneous time of prayer as we joined hands, worshiped God, and lifted up each other's needs to the Lord. It wasn't a forced, unnatural show of "talking about God" so we'd look spiritual; we were merely discussing the most real aspect of our lives—Jesus. What an awesome example of redeemed time! We not only built up each other, we learned how to seek God side by side. And that transparency and ability to discuss spiritual issues will one day sustain our future marriages.

Practice financial responsibility. Not only do we need to learn to make money and support ourselves, we also need to learn how to manage our money responsibly. Now is the time to learn how to budget, save, and tithe consistently.

For several weeks, my parents met with me and two other friends to help us each create personal budgets.

One of our assignments was to record every penny we spent for a week. What a revealing exercise! I was completely unaware of how much money I wasted eating out. Although I still go out, I've now put a limit on how much I can spend on food in a month. Another guy I know found he was investing an inordinate amount of his paycheck from his job at the Gap right back into the company! He cut back his clothing budget and began saving and giving more.

Because we singles don't have as many responsibilities as married folks, we can quickly develop poor habits of spending. We need to make sure we don't develop patterns with money that will jeopardize a marriage or, even more important, waste God's resources.

In addition to learning about budgeting, balancing a checkbook, and car and health insurance, we also need to establish our own philosophy toward finances. What kind of lifestyle does God want us to pursue? What is His view of money and possessions? Left unanswered, these issues can cause serious stress in a marriage and serious regret if we waste our lives pursuing the wrong things.

A book that has helped me tremendously in this area is *Money, Possessions and Eternity* by Randy Alcorn (Tyndale House Pub., Wheaton, IL). Also, Larry Burkett has written excellent books and study guides about practical issues related to finance; many are designed specifically for young adults.

Practice parenthood. Children are not one of the risks of marriage; they are one of the rewards. And the work of becoming a good father or mother starts while we're single. Right now, we can take notes from the veterans and practice those qualities of parenthood we want to model for our future children.

We can use our current relationships to prepare ourselves. God has blessed me with five younger siblings ranging from age two to thirteen. While being a parent is in a totally different league from being a brother, I can "practice" parenthood now by investing time in my siblings' lives, by doing my best to direct them toward godliness, and by including them in my activities. I've changed my share of dirty diapers; I've fed, washed, and clothed my brothers and sisters. In doing so, I've learned a little of the responsibility and joy that accompany parenting.

Look for opportunities to practice and learn now, whether or not you have younger siblings. I'm inspired by Jeanne, a friend of my family's, who takes this preparation seriously. As the youngest in her family, she never had the opportunity to be around small children. To make up for lost time, Jeanne volunteers as a mother's helper free-of-charge for a family with seven kids. One day a week she goes to this family's home and apprentices in all the household's activities, including watching the children, cooking, doing laundry, and cleaning.

Another important part of preparing for parenthood is observing good parents in action. You may or may not have a good dad or mom in your home. If you don't, find parents in your church to follow as examples. One friend told me he tries to observe and spend time with dads who he wants to be like. He asks himself these questions: "How do these godly dads handle discipline? How do they teach and instruct their kids?" Though he doesn't get any college credit for it, I have a feeling his study will pay off when he one day faces the biggest test of manhood: being a dad himself.

Practice practical life skills. What are practical life skills? Just ask your parents to let you take over the maintenance of your house—including shopping, planning menus, and cooking meals for a couple of months—you'll soon find out.

While these sorts of skills aren't glamorous, they are an important part of managing a household. We have no excuse for not preparing ourselves in this area. And the best preparation is actually doing it. A few years ago, my mom had me start doing all the grocery shopping for the family. I also had to cook one dinner each week. At first, I didn't always cook the most appetizing meals for my family, but I got better!

Though I've improved my skills in the kitchen, I'm still woefully unprepared in the area of home maintenance. I'm sure you have your own weak spots too. Let's get to work strengthening them! If you don't know where to start, sit down with your folks or a godly man or woman in your church, and ask them to outline the skills they find necessary to run a household. Write down these skills, and establish a plan to master each one.

MARRIAGE IS NOT THE FINISH LINE!

Perhaps I've struck a chord with you. Maybe you can think of a few ways to redeem your time so that you can feel confident that you're using your singleness for God's glory. What might you put into practice even today?

We all can actively choose ways to prepare ourselves for

marriage, if God wills it for our future. But let's remember the real reasons for our preparation. Preparing for marriage is a byproduct of growing in maturity and Christlikeness. But while marriage is optional, developing Christlike qualities is not. Each of us must develop love, humility, patience, forgiveness, and responsibility.

As singles, part of good stewardship involves gaining the skills we'll need in marriage. But marriage is not the finish line. Statistically speaking, most of us will eventually marry. But we need to make sure we "redeem the time" to glorify God, not to earn brownie points from Him so we can demand marriage. We prepare and develop our characters so we can become as flexible and useful for Him as possible, no matter what he plans for our future. Biological clocks can tick all they want; let's redeem today!

CHAPTER THIRTEEN

Ready for the Sack but Not for the Sacrifice

HOW TO HAVE A BIBLICAL AND REALISTIC VISION OF MARRIAGE

For a year in high school, I operated a small production company, Hizway Wedding Videography, that videotaped weddings. This job was, to say the least, an interesting way to make a living.

An engaged man and woman would contract with me to videotape their wedding so they could remember every last detail of their special day. When that day came, I would arrive at the church several hours early with my camera, lights, tripod, and sound-mixing gear in tow. I then spent the entire day recording, or you might say intruding on, every memorable moment. I captured on tape the ladies fussing over the bride's veil; through the lens I watched the nervous conversation between the groom and his best man. During the ceremony, I recorded the special music, the candle lighting, and the exchanging of vows. At just the right moment, I zoomed in for the kiss.

At the reception, I immortalized images of guests stuffing their faces with appetizers, punch, and those minty candies popular at weddings. Of course, I couldn't miss the cake cutting; the bouquet and garter tosses; or the final event when, amid a shower of birdseed, the couple piled into a waiting car and sped away. (One couple even had me go to the airport to film them boarding a plane for Hawaii...she was still wearing her wedding gown and he, his tuxedo!)

But my real work came *after* the wedding. While the lovebirds enjoyed their honeymoon, I spent my days staring at a monitor, editing many hours' worth of footage down to a seamless, slick, sixty-minute tape. I cut the bloopers and blunders so everything looked perfect.

If you watched one of those videos without knowing all the fast-forwarding and splicing I had done, you could mistakenly believe that the wedding had gone off without a hitch. You wouldn't know that the bride's mother and sister argued fiercely over where to pin the veil or that the tuxedos barely arrived in time or that a nephew stuck his hand in the punch bowl. In an edited video, everything flows naturally, the bride and groom look like stars in their own movie, and the soft background music gives it all the feel of a fairy tale.

It's beautiful and romantic, but it's not reality.

An Edited Vision of Marriage

Unfortunately, many young adults have a view of marriage as limited and unreal as the wedding videos I used to create. These people think of married life as one grand, thrilling moment after another, and the everyday, mundane parts of marriage are safely edited from the picture.

A friend once told me that the girls in her dormitory spent hours poring over bridal magazines. They'd choose their gowns and bridesmaid dresses. They'd endlessly compare engagement rings. My friend was exasperated that these girls devoted so much energy and attention to what is, in reality, a very small

part of marriage. "Marriage is much more than a wedding ceremony," write Gary and Betsy Ricucci in their book *Love that
Lasts*. "A wedding is an event, but a marriage is a state of being.
It's not a one-time act; it's a lifelong commitment to be developed and maintained." One can only hope those girls will give
thought to what comes *after* the wedding festivities. Will they
be prepared for the development and maintenance that marriage will demand?

Girls aren't the only ones guilty of reducing marriage to a
single aspect. We guys have our own immature view of marriage too. I'm ashamed to admit that I struggle with the tendency
to equate marriage with sex. When I picture being married, I
almost immediately picture going to bed with my wife, as if
that's all married people do! Yes, husbands and wives do have
sex, and there's nothing wrong with looking forward to that
important part of married life, but that can't be the extent of my
vision. If I foster the idea of sex as the chief purpose and end of
marriage, I'll one day enter marriage unprepared, and I'll face
certain disappointment. I may be ready for the sack, but am I
ready for the sacrifice of married life?

How about you? Do you find yourself concentrating on one
aspect of marriage to the exclusion of all others? Or can you
maintain the big picture and prepare yourself for all that marriage will be?

DULY CONSIDERING

As singles, we face the important task of cultivating a balanced,
biblical understanding of God's purpose and plan for marriage.
Marriage is not to be, in the words of an old wedding sermon,
"enterprised lightly or wantonly to satisfy man's carnal lusts and
appetites, but reverently, discreetly, advisedly, soberly and in the

fear of God, duly considering the causes for which matrimony was ordained."

How should we view marriage? According to this sermon, reverently, discreetly, advisedly, and soberly. These words, rich in meaning, give us a vivid, vast picture of marriage. *Reverence* means "a profound respect mingled with awe." *Discretion* means "discernment or good judgment." To do something *advisedly* means "to carefully consider" it. And to approach something *soberly* means "to be well-balanced, unaffected by passion, excitement, or prejudice."

Do these qualities define our approach to marriage? All too often, the answer is "no." I've heard people validate the union of two people solely because, in their opinion, the two would have beautiful babies. That may be true, and there's nothing wrong if they do, but if we place importance on such an issue, we obviously don't view marriage very highly. We need to leave behind the giddy idea that marriage is a game or some sort of "prom for grown-ups" in which being a cute couple matters most.

Instead, we need to sober ourselves up with a cold splash of reality. We need to understand God's purpose for marriage as well as our responsibility in marriage. Fortunately, God's Word gives us both in clear terms. The Ricuccis write in *Love that Lasts,* "You don't have to read very far in the Bible to be astounded by God's perspective on this most sacred and significant relationship." Gary and Betsy go on to outline this perspective in their book. They've given me permission to excerpt (and slightly adapt for singles) the section in which they answer the question, "What is marriage?"

Marriage is the first institution (Genesis 2:22–24). It was ordained before the family, before civil government—even before the Church.

Marriage depicts the supernatural union between Jesus and the Church (Ephesians 5:31–32). One of the most beautiful analogies God uses to define his relationship with us is that of a marriage. To grasp this is both inspirational and sobering. People should be able to look at our marriages and say, "So that's what the Church is like? That's what it means to have a relationship with Jesus?"

God intends to cultivate the same abundant, unconditional love between a husband and wife as he himself has for us. Marriage is a profound and marvelous mystery established by God for his glory.

Marriage is the event God has selected to consummate all of time (Revelation 19:7). God has had at least two thousand years to make preparations for honoring his Son at the end of the age. It's significant that God has not scheduled the coronation of the Lamb or the graduation of the Lamb. Instead he has ordained the marriage supper of the Lamb. Why marriage? Because it speaks of union and intimacy as nothing else does. The greatest thing God could plan for Jesus was to present him with his radiant Bride. No wonder we are so deeply moved when a bride walks down the aisle. Marriage is a holy and wonderful gift. And one day we will be called to account for our stewardship of this gift.

Marriage is to be held in honor (Hebrews 13:4). The Amplified Version of the Bible elaborates on this verse, noting that marriage should be esteemed worthy, precious, of great price, and especially dear. This requires that we guard against any thought that dishonors or belittles marriage.

When I (Gary) stop at the grocery store for milk and bread, I will often buy flowers for Betsy. On one particular trip, when I reached the cashier, he joked, "What's the matter—you in the doghouse?" It would have been easy to laugh along with him and join in the joke. But I wanted him to know my marriage was important to me. Here was a chance to challenge his misconception, to sow in his mind a seed of hope about the tremendous potential of marriage. So without getting self-righteous about it, I answered, "No—I just love my wife."

Your future spouse is created in the image of God. Your marriage will be a sacred relationship.

The Ricuccis also say that we should use "every opportunity to defend the sanctity of marriage." Even though the Ricuccis target married couples, I think singles can defend the sanctity of marriage as well.

How can we do this? Earlier, I told you about my friend whose dorm mates' view of marriage went little further than a discussion of engagement rings and wedding gowns. How could my friend have defended the sanctity of marriage in that setting? Without dampening the other girls' enthusiasm for their future weddings (they have every right to be excited about the big day), she could have helped them by gently reminding them of other important aspects of married life. She could have asked questions such as "How are you going to raise your kids? How are you going to keep the communication lines open with your husband?" These kinds of questions can encourage proper perspective and balance in our view of marriage.

In my case, the next time a group of my male friends begins to discuss marriage as merely the opportunity to have sex, I can, once I've adjusted my own attitude, challenge their limited and immature view. Even though I'm single, I can help myself and others to have a high view of marriage by rejecting attitudes and words that belittle or reduce it from the place of honor God has given it.

How can *you* encourage others to hold marriage in high esteem?

THE CRUCIBLE OF MARRIAGE

The Ricuccis' final point needs our extra attention. They write:

> *Marriage is a refining process.* Conflict will occur in every marriage. When issues erupt between the two of you, it will be easy for one to blame the other. "If you would just leave the air conditioner on when it gets this hot, I wouldn't get upset!" The fact is, your spouse won't make you sin. They simply reveal what's already in your heart. One of the best wedding gifts God will give you is a full-length mirror called your spouse. If He were to attach a card it would say, "Here's to helping you discover what you're really like. Congratulations!"

From a distance, singles see the glow of married life and think only of how it will warm them. And in many ways it will. But we forget that God wants to use the fire of marriage to not only comfort us, but refine and cleanse us from our selfishness and sin. We come to warm our hands by the fire of marriage; God wants to throw us into it!

I don't want to give (or believe!) the idea that marriage will be all pain and discomfort. But marriage won't be unending bliss and personal fulfillment either, and if we don't realize this, our experience of marriage will be extremely uncomfortable. Mike Mason, in his book *The Mystery of Marriage,* writes: "Holy matrimony, like other holy orders, was never intended as a comfort station for lazy people. On the contrary, it is a systematic program of deliberate and thoroughgoing self-sacrifice... Marriage is really a drastic course of action...It is a radical step and is not intended for anyone who is not prepared, indeed eager, to surrender his own will and to be wholeheartedly submissive to the will of another."

As quickly as possible, we must dispel any selfish notions that marriage is about what we can get instead of what we can give.

THE FINE PRINT OF DREAMS

Advice columnist Ann Landers once gave some helpful advice regarding the work marriage involves. One of her readers lamented the unrealistic ideas many girls had of marriage, beseeching, "Why don't you level with them, Ann?" Landers replied:

I have leveled with the girls—from Anchorage to
    Amarillo.
I tell them that all marriages are happy.
It's the living together afterward that's tough.
I tell them that a good marriage is not a gift,
It's an achievement.
That marriage is not for kids. It takes guts and maturity.
It separates the men from the boys and the women from
    the girls.
I tell them that marriage is tested daily by the ability to
    compromise.
Its survival can depend on being smart enough to know

what's worth fighting about. Or making an issue of
or even mentioning.
Marriage is giving—and more important, it's forgiving.
And it is almost always the wife who must do these
things.
Then, as if that were not enough, she must be willing to
forget what she forgave.
Often that is the hardest part.
Oh, I have leveled all right.
If they don't get my message, Buster,
It's because they don't want to get it.
Rose-colored glasses are never made in bifocals
Because nobody wants to read the small print in dreams.

In our daydreams about marriage, we too often forget what a drastic course of action marriage really is. We read the captivating headlines but neglect to read the exacting fine print. What does the fine print say? That good marriages require work, patience, self-discipline, sacrifice, and submission. That successful marriages take "guts and maturity" and, we should add, a biblical understanding of God's purpose and plan for it. Only when we cultivate these qualities and disciplines can we carry out our responsibilities and experience true joy and fulfillment in marriage.

MAN ENOUGH TO ANSWER

I want to close this chapter with a challenge to young men. While Ann Landers' advice to girls calls them to awaken from childish dreams and realize that marriage takes work, the following poem, entitled "A Woman's Question" by Lena Lathrop, speaks particularly to men. It still chills me every time I read it.

Lathrop's words show me to be the immature boy that I am, stopping me in my tracks and daring me to be man enough to treat a woman right. Some of the poem's wording might seem old-fashioned, but the message is timeless.

Do you know you have asked for the costliest thing
Ever made by the Hand above?
A woman's heart, and a woman's life—
And a woman's wonderful love.

Do you know you have asked for this priceless thing
As a child might ask for a toy?
Demanding what others have died to win,
With the reckless dash of a boy.

You have written my lesson of duty out,
Manlike, you have questioned me.
Now stand at the bars of my woman's soul
Until I shall question thee.

You require your mutton shall always be hot,
Your socks and your shirt be whole;
I require your heart be true as God's stars
And as pure as His heaven your soul.

You require a cook for your mutton and beef,
I require a far greater thing;
A seamstress you're wanting for socks and shirts—
I look for a man and a king.

A king for the beautiful realm called Home,
And a man that his Maker, God,

Shall look upon as He did on the first
And say: "It is very good."

I am fair and young, but the rose may fade
From this soft young cheek one day;
Will you love me then 'mid the falling leaves,
As you did 'mong the blossoms of May?

Is your heart an ocean so strong and true,
I may launch my all on its tide?
A loving woman finds heaven or hell
On the day she is made a bride.

I require all things that are grand and true,
All things that a man should be;
If you give this all, I would stake my life
To be all you demand of me.

If you cannot be this, a laundress and cook
You can hire and little to pay;
But a woman's heart and a woman's life
Are not to be won that way.

To girls reading this book, I pray this poem serves as a reminder to keep your standards high. Require all things that are "grand and true." As you consider the possibility of marriage, don't lower your standards for a moment; any guy who asks you to do so isn't worth your time.

And to the guys, we have our work cut out for us, don't we? My hope for us is that we would truly grasp the costliness, the pricelessness, of a woman's love. It is no small thing, no game, to invite a girl to accompany us through life. May we earn the right to make such a request by striving to be men of integrity—men whose hearts are oceans "strong and true." Then, and only then, should we stand at the bars of a woman's soul and ask to gain entrance.

CHAPTER FOURTEEN

What Matters at Fifty?

CHARACTER QUALITIES AND ATTITUDES
THAT MATTER MOST IN A LIFE PARTNER

A s I ponder the foreverness of marriage, one question keeps rattling through my mind: "What qualities should I look for in a wife?" Perhaps you wonder the same thing as you consider spending the rest of your life with one special person. What would make someone the perfect mate for you?

When I think of that question, I know the answer entails many deep, internal characteristics, but in everyday life, I still find it difficult to get past the superficial. A cute girl walks in the room, and all my common sense evaporates. How many times have I made a complete fool of myself by falling head over heels for someone simply because of her charm and beauty? Too many times.

To cure this tendency, I've created a little game. When I meet a beautiful girl and I'm tempted to be overly impressed by her external features, I try to imagine what this girl will look like when she is fifty years old. (If this girl is with her mother, this game doesn't take too much imagination.) This girl may be young and pretty now, but what happens when the beauty fades? Does anything within her beckon to me? Is it her character that radiates and draws me toward her, or is it just the fact that her summer dress shows off a little too much of her tan? So what if her feminine outline captures my eye today? When pregnancies add stretch marks and the years add extra pounds, will something in this girl's soul continue to attract me?

THINGS THAT LAST

As we consider what's important in a marriage partner, we need to get past the surface issues of looks, dress, and performance in front of others. "The LORD does not look at the things man looks at," God says. "Man looks at the outward appearance, but the LORD looks at the heart" (1 Samuel 16:7). Proverbs 31:30 tells us, "Charm is deceptive, and beauty is fleeting..." The same verse tells us that the kind of person who deserves praise is the one who "fears the LORD."

We're too easily impressed by image; God wants us to value qualities that will last. Wisely choosing a marriage partner requires that we get back to the essentials of a person's character and attitude.

In this chapter we'll look at the character qualities and attitudes important in a spouse. But as we do so, we also want to ask, "Am I cultivating these in my own life?" Let's be careful to maintain a humble attitude of self-examination. We need to not only concentrate on *finding* the right person but, more important, on *becoming* the right person ourselves.

CHARACTER

"Character is what you are in the dark when no one but God is watching," writes Randy Alcorn. "Anyone can look good in front of an audience, or even in front of their friends," he continues. "It's an entirely different thing to stand naked before God, to be known as you truly are on the inside." We don't define a person's true character by the image that person wishes to convey or the reputation he or she hides behind, but by the choices and decisions that person has made and makes each day.

It takes real wisdom to observe a person's character. It also takes time. William Davis writes, "Your reputation is learned in an hour; your character does not come to light for a year."

GLIMPSES OF TRUE CHARACTER

How do we evaluate a person's character? How do we get past image and reputation to catch a glimpse of who a person really is?

As we evaluate someone's character (including our own), we need to carefully observe three areas—how the individual relates to God, the way he or she treats others, and the way this person disciplines his or her personal life. These areas are like windows into a person's character. "As the daylight can be seen through very small holes, so little things will illustrate a person's character," writes Samuel Smiles. "Indeed, character consists in little acts, well and honorably performed."

Let's look at some of the "little acts" that can tell us more about a person.

1. How a Person Relates to God

A person's relationship to God is the defining relationship in his or her life—when this relationship is out of order, every other relationship will suffer. Scripture plainly states that a Christian should not even consider a non-Christian for a spouse. "Don't team up with those who are unbelievers," the Bible says (2 Corinthians 6:14, NLT). Both you and the person you marry must have a dynamic, growing, personal relationship with Jesus Christ. The question is not merely "Are you and a potential spouse saved?" but rather "Are both of you in love with Jesus Christ? Will you place Him even before each other?"

"This is one of those beautiful paradoxes of biblical truth," write David Powlison and John Yenchko. "If you love and want your spouse more than anything, you will end up selfish, fearful, bitter, or disillusioned. If you love Jesus more than anything else, you will really love and enjoy your spouse. You will be someone worth marrying!"

Once in a conversation about relationships, two Christian girls told me that they find focus on God one of the most attractive qualities in a guy. "It's obvious when he really loves the Lord," my friend Sarah said. "When he's telling you about his love for God, you can tell that he's not distracted by you."

"Exactly!" affirmed Jayme. "It's funny because the guys that really go out of their way to impress girls don't impress me at all. They make me nauseated."

Look for, and work on becoming, a man or woman who, as a single, seeks God wholeheartedly, putting Him before anything else. Don't worry about impressing the opposite sex. Instead, strive to please and glorify God. Along the way you'll catch the attention of people with the same priorities.

2. How a Person Relates to Others

The second window to a person's character is his or her relationships with others. Watch how a potential partner (and you) relate to the following people:

Authorities. How does a potential mate respond to people in authority? Does this person respect the authority of a boss or pastor even if he or she disagrees with that authority figure? A guy who can't follow legitimate orders will have difficulty holding a job or receiving pastoral correction when needed. A girl who can't respect a teacher's or coach's authority will have difficulty honoring her husband. Look for, and strive to become, a person who respects God-given authority.

Parents. You've probably heard this sage advice before: "The way a guy treats his mom is the way he'll treat his wife." It's true. The same goes for the way a girl relates to her dad. I'm not saying that a person who has had a bad relationship with his or her dad or mom can't have a good marriage. By God's grace we can overcome old patterns. But we do need to ask, "If he can't be loving and gentle with his mom, why should I believe he'll be loving and gentle with me as his wife?" or "If she can't respect her dad, will she be able to respect me as her husband?"

Don't forget to evaluate your own life. How do you relate to your parents? Can you improve the way you interact with them so you'll know how to honor your future spouse? If you'd *really* like the answer to these questions, ask your parents to tell you their perspectives on your relationship with them.

The opposite sex. There's a huge difference between genuine friendliness and flirtatiousness. Learn to distinguish between the two. No one wants to marry a flirt. Guys, if a girl flits like a butterfly from one guy to the next, always in need of male attention, do you really think marriage will suddenly change her? Girls, do you want to marry a man with a wandering eye? And what about yourself? Where do you stand on the friendly-flirtatious scale? Do you need to change your attitudes and actions toward members of the opposite sex?

Companions. A person's companions are the people who influence and shape him or her. In this category, the *way* someone treats his or her friends is not as important as *who* these friends are. A. W. Tozer observed, "There is a law of moral attraction that draws every man to the society most like himself.

Where we go when we are free to go where we will is a near-infallible index of character."

Who are a potential marriage partner's closest friends? How do these friends act? What do they value? If they're caught up in partying and living recklessly, the person who spends time with them will probably share those pursuits. What about your companions? Are you pursuing relationships with people who encourage you in your walk with the Lord? Or do your friends drag you down? Don't underestimate how much your close friends shape your character.

3. Personal Discipline
The third window to character is how a person disciplines and conducts his or her personal life. "Habit," writes Charlotte Mason, "is the greater part of nature." The things we do involuntarily, almost without thinking, reveal our character.

When we consider this category, we need to note the difference between sinful habits and simply annoying habits or poor manners. Everyone has habits that another person will find silly or irritating. My dad drives my mother crazy with the way he eats corn on the cob. His method is reminiscent of an old typewriter: Munch, munch, munch, munch, kaching! Munch, munch, munch down the next row. This may not be the best table manners, but it isn't a sinful habit. Instead of concerning ourselves with issues such as these, we need to examine whether a potential spouse (or we ourselves) fosters habits that are disobedient to God or revealing of a deeper disregard for others.

The following are a few areas in which a person's habits give us a glimpse into his or her character. Watch these closely in your own life, too.

How a person uses time. I heard Elisabeth Elliot give a speech in which she said that one of the things that first attracted her to Jim Elliot was the fact that he memorized Scripture as he waited in the cafeteria line. That observation told her that Jim was disciplined and efficient.

The way a person spends his or her leisure time tells us what he or she values. Does this person fill free time with mindless hours in front of the TV? Does this person cultivate his or her mind and build relationships, or does he or she run to the next distraction? Seek to find someone (and to be the kind of person) who uses time wisely.

How he or she handles money. The way a person handles money is one, if not the surest, indicator of character. At his nineteenth birthday party, my friend Andy asked people to bring money. But he didn't want the money for himself. Instead, he gave all of it to a Christian outreach effort in the inner city. Andy's attitude toward material things proved him a man of compassion, love, and generosity. It showed that he valued the eternal more than the material.

Is the person you're observing (or are you) caught up in clothing, cars, and other material things? Does this person think through purchases, or does he or she spend impulsively, prone to splurging? A person's spending habits reveal his or her level of responsibility.

How he or she takes care of his or her body. We should not fault a person because of things he or she cannot control—height, features, and in some cases weight. Neither should we be overly concerned with the external. However, the way a person cares for his or her body tells us something about that person's character.

First, how does this person dress? A girl who dresses immodestly may catch guys' attention, but what does her clothing say about her heart? A guy who spends his money on the latest style may have the appearance of "togetherness," but his infatuation with fashion could mean he's too preoccupied with what people think of him (and that he may make poor decisions with his money).

Next, how does this person care for his or her body? Does he or she have self-disciplined eating habits? Does he or she have a reasonable and consistent program of staying fit? God wants us to maintain the health and condition of our bodies so that we can more effectively serve Him. This does not mean, however, that we should become obsessed with exercise. A person who is too concerned about weight lifting is just as out of balance as the person who doesn't exercise at all.

How would *you* stand up to evaluation in this category? Is there room for improvement in your life?

THE IMPACT OF ATTITUDE

Attitude is the second essential criteria in choosing a spouse. Attitude is a person's vantage point, the way he or she looks at and reacts to life. For the Christian, this involves more than mere positive thinking. A godly attitude involves God-centered, Bible-based thinking—working to view ourselves, others, and our circumstances from God's perspective.

The following are a few key ways that godly attitudes are expressed:

An attitude of willing obedience to God. As you seek a mate, look for someone who will listen and act without hesitation to what God is telling him or her. You want someone with an attitude like David's, saying to God, "I will hurry, without lingering, to obey your commands" (Psalm 119:60, NLT). An attitude of willing obedience recognizes the lordship of Jesus in every area of life. Is the person you're interested in consistently looking for ways to submit more of his or her life to God? Does he

or she work to overcome bad habits? Is this person being con-
formed to today's culture, or does he or she push against it,
seeking to be transformed into Christ's image?

Are you working to develop an obedient attitude in your
own life? You'll never be perfect or find a perfect mate—we're
all sinners—but only people with an attitude of willing obedience to God's Word will continue to grow in godliness and
maturity throughout their lives.

An attitude of humility. An attitude of humility considers others' needs first. The Bible states, "Do nothing out of selfish ambi-
tion or vain conceit, but in humility consider others better than
yourselves" (Philippians 2:3). Does the person you're observing
place the needs of others before his or her own? Watch the small
things. When he's on the basketball court, how does he act?
Even in competition does he seek to serve others? How does she
respond when conflict arises in her family? Is she quick to
blame the other party or humble enough to share blame and
seek resolution? And how do *you* handle these situations?

One of the things I respect most about my dad is his willingness to humble himself before my mom and the rest of my
family by confessing sin. If he has spoken a harsh word or acted
uncaringly, he doesn't hesitate to seek forgiveness. A lesser man
can't do this.

Two people don't keep a marriage strong because they never
make mistakes; they keep a marriage strong by maintaining an
attitude of humility that is quick to confess sin, put the other
first, and seek forgiveness.

An attitude of industriousness. Don't judge a person by his or
her line of work, but do take note of the attitude with which
this person approaches work. An attitude of industriousness is
one of willingness to work hard at whatever task presents itself.
Bill Bennett writes: "Work...is not what we do *for* a living but

what we do *with* our living...The opposite of work is not leisure or play or having fun but idleness—not *investing* ourselves in anything."

In Proverbs 31:17 the noble wife is described as someone who "sets about her work vigorously; her arms are strong for her tasks." (Of course industriousness is important for both men and women.) Look for someone who energetically invests his or her life in something important right now. Strive for this attitude in yourself, too.

An attitude of contentment and hopefulness. An attitude of contentment and hopefulness is one that recognizes God's sovereignty in every situation. It is faith-birthed optimism that looks to God—an attitude more aware of and grateful for the evidence of God's grace than of problems needing correction.

Here are a few important questions to ask about the person you're observing as well as about yourself: Does this person have complaint or praise on his or her lips? Does he or she nit-pick at the faults of others or consistently encourage? Does this person view his or her circumstances with a spirit of hopelessness, or does he or she remain confident of God's faithfulness?

Early in his marriage, the Reverend E. V. Hill and his wife, Jane, faced financial difficulty. He had foolishly invested in a service station, and the business had failed. Money was very tight. Dr. Dobson, who heard Reverend Hill share their story at Jane's funeral, recounts it this way:

Shortly after the fiasco with the service station, E. V. came home one night and found the house dark. When he opened the door, he saw that Jane had prepared a candlelight dinner for two.

"What meaneth thou this?" he said with characteristic humor.

"Well," said Jane, "we're going to eat by candlelight tonight."

E. V. thought that was a great idea and went into the bathroom to wash his hands. He tried unsuccessfully to turn on the light. Then he felt his way into the bedroom and flipped another switch. Darkness prevailed. The young pastor went back to the dining room and asked Jane why the electricity was off. She began to cry.

"You work so hard, and we're trying," said Jane, "but it's pretty rough. I didn't have quite enough money to pay the light bill. I didn't want you to know about it, so I thought we would just eat by candlelight."

Dr. Hill described his wife's words with intense emotion: "She could have said, 'I've never been in this situation before. I was reared in the home of Dr. Caruthers, and we never had our lights cut off.' She could have broken my spirit; she could have ruined me; she could have demoralized me. But instead she said, 'Somehow or another we'll get these lights on. But let's eat tonight by candlelight.'"

Tears come to my eyes every time I read this story. Mrs. Hill's optimism and readiness to walk through tough times with her husband exemplify the two qualities I desire in my own life and pray for most in a wife. I'm looking for someone who will light candles, not just curse the darkness.

THE CLIFF

I've shared all these characteristics and attitudes in hopes of clarifying what really matters in a spouse—what to look for in another person and what to work on in our own lives. We should not use these qualities to bash the opposite sex or as an excuse to avoid marriage. No one will achieve perfection in all the areas we've explored. For the man who expects to find someone who is perfect, Benjamin Tillett had this quip: "God help the man who won't marry until he finds the perfect woman, and God help him still more if he finds her."

We will never find the perfect spouse. If we did, why would he or she want to marry an imperfect person like you or me? Benjamin Franklin said, "Keep your eyes wide open before marriage—half shut afterward." Marriage requires faith in God's provision and a willingness to forgive imperfections—the mercy needed to keep our eyes "half shut" to the flaws.

One young guy e-mailed me about his fear regarding marriage: "How can I possibly get to know a person well enough before marriage to know if they're right? It seems like getting married is like jumping off a cliff." In one sense he's right. Marriage will always be a step of faith. Not a blind leap, but a step just beyond what we can see for certain.

My pastor, C. J. Mahaney, tells the humorous story of how, before his wedding, he reached out his hand to his father-in-law-to-be and said, "Thank you, sir, for trusting me with your daughter." The man replied, "I don't trust you." Then after a long pause he said, "I trust God." This father had his trust in the right place.

We can't trust ourselves, and we can't completely know the person we decide to marry, but we *can* trust God to guide us in our decisions and to help us follow through with our commitments.

True Beauty

While single, I'm working to build godly character in my life and have the right attitudes. And as I observe the young ladies around me, I'm keeping my eyes wide open. And, yes, I'm still playing my little game of asking, "What matters at fifty?" It helps me look past the fleeting issues of youth and beauty and focus on the essentials of character and attitude.

Poor girls, if they had any idea about my game... But then, who knows? Maybe they've been imagining what I'll look like at fifty. Now there's a scary thought!

One of these days, and this is the moment for which I'm hoping and praying, I'm going to meet a girl, and when I imagine her at fifty she'll be even more beautiful than she is today. The years won't detract; they'll only sharpen and mature her. Because with a woman who fears God, whose inner strength draws from the wellspring of His life, time can only add to her true beauty. Of course, the signs of age will emerge, but the spirit which lights up her sparkling eyes will still be young, vibrant, and alive. That's what I want to grow to love.

What will I do when I meet this young woman? I think about that often. I don't know exactly what I'll say. Maybe I'll get down on my knees and beg her to spend the rest of her life growing old with me. We can watch our bodies fall apart and together wait for the day when the Master gives us new ones.

And when I kiss her on our wedding day, I'll revel in the wife of my youth, but I'll whisper in her ear, "I can't wait to see you when you're fifty."

CHAPTER FIFTEEN

Principled Romance

PRINCIPLES THAT CAN GUIDE YOU FROM FRIENDSHIP TO MATRIMONY

J ason and Shelly *still* debate over when they first met. One Thursday night after the college group's Bible study, Jason walked up and introduced himself.

"How are you?" Jason asked as he stuck out his hand to greet Shelly. "My name's Jason. I've seen you around but never had a chance to meet you."

The dark-haired girl smiled and said, "I'm Shelly, and actually we have met before; you just don't remember."

"No way," Jason said, a little embarrassed. "Are you sure?"

"Oh, I'm sure," she said with a good-natured laugh. "It was earlier this spring. You were sitting in front of me one Sunday, and somebody introduced us briefly. That's okay; I'm easy to forget."

"That's impossible!" he protested. "I'm sure I'd remember you if we'd met."

The playful little argument paved the way for an ongoing friendship. Whenever Jason saw Shelly, he'd walk up to her and say, "Hi, I'm Jason. I don't think we've met before." That always brought a laugh.

Over the next few months, Jason and Shelly began to get to

know each other better. Since they had the same circle of friends, they'd often end up at Shari's restaurant with a group of guys and girls after church. The college students would spend hours talking and laughing over cup after cup of coffee. Shelly always drank tea. Jason took note of that. And it wasn't the only thing he was taking note of. He was discovering the depth of her personality. Shelly was quiet, but when she did speak, she said thoughtful and intelligent things. Shelly knew how to have fun, and she knew when to be serious. And at church, Jason could almost always find Shelly serving or helping someone else. On Sundays she volunteered in the nursery, and in the college group many girls sought out Shelly for advice and comfort.

Shelly was doing her own reconnaissance work on Jason. She noted his smile and the kindness he showed to everyone, whether or not they were popular or could do anything for him in return. She was impressed with his authentic relationship with God; he didn't just put on a show. And she liked the fact that they could relate to each other as brother and sister.

Shelly liked being around Jason. Could they possibly become more than friends someday? She decided not to worry about that yet.

Unbeknown to Shelly, Jason *was* worrying about it. Or at least spending a considerable amount of time thinking about it. As he got to know Shelly, he kept checking off, one-by-one, the items on his "wish list" of qualities for a wife. Jason found himself thinking about Shelly during the day and looking forward to the next time he'd see her. "I can't get this girl out of my head," he prayed one night as he tossed in bed, trying to fall asleep. "Lord, Shelly is everything I've ever wanted in a girl. What do I do next?"

No Formulas

What do you do when you think you've met the person you want to marry? Friendship is great, but how should you proceed from there? How do you get to know that special person better?

The Bible doesn't provide a one-size-fits-all program for moving from friendship to marriage. Our lives are too different, our circumstances too unique, and our God too creative to have only one formula for romance. The various ways in which God brings men and women together, like the unique designs of snowflakes, are never quite the same. But just as a one-of-a-kind snowflake can only form at a specific temperature and precipitation, a God-honoring romance can only form when we follow godly patterns and principles.

In this chapter, I'd like to outline a new pattern for relationships that can help us avoid the problems often encountered in dating. The stages I propose are not a magic solution to these problems, nor are they the only way for romance to unfold. But I think they can help us develop godly romantic relationships. These stages are: *casual friendship—deeper friendship—purposeful intimacy with integrity—engagement.*

Let's examine a few helpful principles that can guide us through the "Now what?" questions of relationships. As we do, we'll see the four stages of God-honoring romance at play. The first principle applies to stage 1.

1. *Remember your relational responsibilities.*
Imagine you're in a car on a lonely desert road. No one's in sight, and the smooth pavement stretches out as far as you can see. You know the vehicle can go fast; you just don't know how fast. But you'd like to find out. No one will see you; why not try

it? You throw the car into high gear and roar down the road.

Now imagine you're in the car again, but this time a dear friend sits in the passenger seat. And instead of being on a deserted road, you're in the heart of a busy city, surrounded by other cars and pedestrians. Then out of the corner of your eye, you see a police car. You don't even *think* of speeding. You drive down the street slowly and carefully.

What was the difference between the two scenarios? The difference is that in the first you were an isolated person who only had yourself to worry about. But the second scenario placed you in relationships with others. Instead of being alone, you had responsibilities. If you wrecked the car, you would be responsible for the life of the person strapped in the seat next to you. Your recklessness would also place the lives of the motorists around you in danger. And finally, the policeman's presence reminded you of the traffic laws you should obey. You drove slowly.

The same principle works in romantic relationships. If you start out thinking only of yourself—Will this person like me? Would he or she make a good husband or wife for me?—you'll speed into a relationship too quickly and probably run over people along the way. But if you remember that your actions affect others, you'll find the resolve to proceed cautiously and carefully.

Every time you feel attracted to someone, keep in mind that you're involved in three kinds of relationships: your relationship with the person you're interested in; your relationships with the people around you, including family and friends; and most important, your relationship with God. You have a responsibility toward each.

Talking to Myself

I try to remember these three relational responsibilities when I find myself interested in a girl. In the early stages of attraction, I have a difficult time remaining clearheaded. I have to immediately remind myself of my responsibilities. I usually end up having a conversation with myself that goes something like this:

"Josh, what's your relationship to this girl?"

"She's a sister in Christ whom I'm instructed to treat with absolute purity."

"Exactly! She's not just a pretty face or a potential wife!"

"No, she's a child of God. God has a plan for her. He's shaping her and molding her into something special."

"So what is your responsibility to her?"

"My responsibility is to make sure I don't get in the way of what God is doing. I should encourage her to keep her focus and dependence on God."

"Okay, good. Now to whom is your second responsibility?"

"My second responsibility is to the people around me."

"Such as..."

"Such as the people in the church group, non-Christians who might observe our relationship, and even my little brothers, who watch how I relate to girls."

"Why do you have to care what they think?"

"I have a responsibility to keep the unity of the group here at church; I have a responsibility to model the love of Jesus to outsiders; and I have a responsibility to set an example for other believers."

"And your primary responsibility is to God, correct?"

"Exactly. I am responsible to keep my way pure, serve others as Christ did, and love my neighbors as I love myself."

These kinds of questions can help us gain a proper perspective right from the start and can determine whether a relationship will be God-honoring or merely self-satisfying. Breaking out of the defective patterns of typical dating requires that we stop seeing ourselves as the "center of the universe" with other people revolving around our desires. Before we embark on a relationship, we need to sober ourselves up by reviewing our relational responsibilities.

2. Seek a deeper friendship first (stage 2).

One spring my four-year-old sister was so excited to see the first flowers pushing out of the soil that she plucked a handful of the unopened buds and proudly gave them to my mother. My mother was disappointed by my sister's impatience. "You picked them too soon," she said. "They're a lot prettier when they're allowed to bloom."

We're often guilty of the same impatience in our relationships. Instead of waiting until friendship fully blooms, we rush into romance. Our impatience not only costs us the beauty of friendship as singles, it can also place our future marriages on shaky ground. Strong marriages are built on a solid foundation of the mutual respect, appreciation, and camaraderie of friendship.

When we find ourselves attracted to someone, we need to make building a deeper friendship our first priority. Too often we believe that relating in a romantic, exclusive relationship will automatically mean we'll be closer and know each other better. But this doesn't always happen. Although romance can be a more exciting level of relationship, it can also foster illusion and infatuation, obscuring the true character of each person involved. Remember, as soon as we unleash our emotions in romantic love, our objectivity begins to fade. For this reason, we need to focus on developing a closer friendship with a potential partner before introducing romance.

Friendship-Deepening Activities

The first priority for a guy and girl is to get to know each other better as individuals—to gain an accurate, unbiased view of each other's true nature. How can you do this? First, instead of dropping out of your regular routines to spend time together, look for opportunities to include one another in your real lives. Find activities that pull you both into each other's world of family, friends, and work, as well as areas of service and ministry.

For Jason, a Spanish major, this meant inviting Shelly to visit the Spanish church he helped translate for one Sunday a month. This activity gave her a glimpse into Jason's love for the Spanish language and the Hispanic people. Another time, Shelly asked Jason to help her teach a Sunday school class for fifth graders. Although they spent the majority of their time in groups during both activities, Jason and Shelly discovered more about each other and deepened their friendship.

Things to Avoid

While your friendship progresses, avoid saying and doing things that express romantic love. The context of a deepening friendship is not the time to talk about your possible future together; it's the time to get to know each other, serve God together in the church, and listen for God's leading. Don't take things into your own hands by flirting or dropping hints about your romantic feelings. And don't encourage your friends to talk about you or to treat you as a couple. When your friends do this, simply invite others to join you in your activities so you can keep from being paired off.

It will take patience and self-control not to express your

feelings prematurely, but it's worth it. "I want you to promise me..." says the maiden in Song of Songs 8:4 (NLT), "not to awaken love until it is ready." The Wycliffe Bible Commentary says, "Love should not be stirred up before its proper time, because the love relationship, unless carefully guarded, may cause grief instead of the great joy it should bring to the human heart." Proverbs 29:20 states, "Do you see a man who speaks in haste? There is more hope for a fool than for him." Don't play the fool in your relationships by speaking too soon. If you're pursuing a deeper friendship, the other person will already have an idea that you're interested, and you can't avoid this. But expressing these feelings in words often "awakens love" before it's ready.

If you really think about it, the need to blurt out our feelings is usually motivated by selfishness, not by a desire to enhance the other person's life. We want to know if our feelings are reciprocated, and we can't bear not knowing how the other person feels. This kind of selfishness not only has the potential to destroy the delicate beginnings of a relationship, it can also make us feel like fools later if our feelings change. You'll never regret the decision to wait to express your feelings.

3. Watch, wait, and pray.
"Want some coffee?" That was Shelly's code-phrase to her mom that meant, "We need to have a serious mother-daughter conversation." Her mom was only too happy to sip on a raspberry mocha at Starbucks and listen as Shelly talked about her feelings for Jason and the questions beginning to race around in her mind. What did he think about her? Did he view her just as a pal? What if he did want something more? Could she picture them together? married?

Shelly's tea got cold as she talked. After she had talked herself ragged and answered most of her own questions, her mom gently reminded her to keep her heart in God's hands. Then her mom had some practical suggestions. Shelly's mom felt it would be good to plan a few get-togethers at their house with other friends so she and Shelly's dad could get to know Jason in a relaxed atmosphere with no pressure. Shelly liked the idea. They closed their "coffee talk" in prayer.

One of the most confusing times in a relationship comes when both the guy and the girl question whether or not to move beyond friendship. While the right time for deepening the relationship varies among couples, we can all benefit from patience. It's always wise to take the extra time to get to know the other person better as a friend and to seek God's guidance.

Unlike Shelly, Jason didn't have the benefit of having his family nearby. He was away at college, and his folks were divorced. So Jason wrote his uncle, his mom's older brother and a strong Christian, a nine-page letter describing Shelly and asking his uncle's advice. Uncle James had always looked out for Jason and acted as a sort of mentor in his life. "Am I crazy to even be thinking about this?" he asked James. His uncle called a week later and prayed with Jason about the situation. And Uncle James asked Jason some tough questions: Was Jason prepared to take care of a wife? Had he talked with the pastor about it? Was he attracted to Shelly's looks or her character? Finally, Uncle James encouraged Jason to wait a month or so and observe Shelly. "You don't need to rush," he said. "If it's God's will, it will all unfold at the right time. It won't hurt to wait."

If you feel inclined to deepen a relationship with a special guy or girl, wait on God through prayer. Seek the counsel of a few trusted, older Christians. Ideally, these people should include your parents, a Christian mentor, and other trusted Christian friends. Ask these people to join you in prayer about this person. Invite them to keep you accountable about the relationship and to point out any "blind spots" in yourself and the person in whom you're interested.

Questions to Ask

During this watching and waiting time, both the guy and girl need to ask themselves tough questions such as "Based on the character I've observed in our friendship, would I consider marrying this person? Am I prepared to move this relationship beyond friendship to pursue marriage?"

Obviously these are very serious questions. Most of the problems we've seen in dating result from people taking these questions too lightly. As a result, people date those they would never consider marrying and pursue romantic relationships merely for fun, not because they're ready for commitment. We can avoid the problems resulting from the "dating mentality" only by waiting on God and refusing to pursue romance until we have the go-ahead from four "green lights":

Green Light 1: God's Word

Based on Scripture, is marriage right for you and the person you're interested in? God established marriage, but He also created boundaries around it. For example, if the person you're thinking about isn't a Christian or has a questionable faith, stop in your tracks. Scripture also warns that some ministries are better carried out by singles; perhaps this truth applies to God's plan for your life. Before proceeding in a relationship, seek God's guidance through His written Word.

Green Light 2: You're Ready for Marriage

Do you have the balanced, realistic vision of married life that we talked about in chapter 13? Are you aware of and ready for the responsibilities of being a husband or wife? Have you reached a level of spiritual maturity and emotional stability as a single that warrants stepping into a lifelong commitment? Are you ready financially? You need to honestly answer these kinds of questions before proceeding with a relationship.

Green Light 3: The Approval and Support of Your Parents or Guardians, Christian Mentors, and Godly Christian Friends

If you think you're ready for marriage, but no one else who knows and loves you agrees, you should probably reconsider. You want the wisdom and viewpoint of those who care about you and can view you objectively. This is not to say that parents or other advisors can never be wrong, but rarely should we proceed without their support and blessing.

Green Light 4: God's Peace

Finally, you can't replace the peace that comes from walking in God's will. When you pray to God or talk with parents and other Christians, does the idea of marriage feel right, or is it marked by tension and apprehension? While I'm not suggesting that you base this important decision on feelings, your feelings can be an added indicator of whether or not you should proceed. Most often you'll feel God's peace only when the previous three green lights are in place.

4. *Define the relationship's purpose: pursuing marriage (stage 3).*
Assuming you've gotten all four green lights, you'll face a time when you need to clearly define the purpose and direction of the relationship.

Remember the first habit of defective dating? "Dating leads to intimacy but not necessarily commitment." Restated, many dating relationships, even serious ones, wander without a clear purpose.

They're stuck in the twilight zone between recreational dating and engagement. Neither person knows exactly what the other is thinking. "Are we dating just for fun, or is this serious? What's our commitment?" We want to avoid this state of limbo. Doing so will require honesty and courage on the part of both people.

Principle 4 applies specifically to the guys, who I believe should be the ones to "make the first move." Please don't misunderstand this as a chauvinistic attitude. Men, we're not to lord anything over girls; that's the exact opposite of the Christlike servanthood husbands must show their wives. But the Bible clearly defines the importance of a man's spiritual leadership in marriage (Ephesians 5:23–25), and I believe part of that leadership should begin in this stage of the relationship. The girls I talk to, Christian and non-Christians alike, agree. They *want* the guy to take the lead and provide direction for the relationship.

So, how should this happen? I believe the man needs to say something such as "We're growing closer in friendship, and I need to be upfront about my motives. With your parents' permission, I want to explore the possibility of marriage. I'm not interested in playing the game of being boyfriend and girlfriend. I'm ready to be tested by you, your family, and those who are responsible for you. My desire is to win your heart."

"But," you might think, "that's so serious." Yes, it is! A woman's heart and future are not things to toy with. That's why the vagueness and squirming on the part of men when it's time to "get serious or get lost" is so reprehensible. There comes a point, gentlemen, when we need to be bold, and I'm sorry to say, too often we lack that boldness. We've lost the concept of chivalry. We do girls a great disservice by first pursuing romance before we're ready to commit, and then by hesitating when we should commit. Enough is enough! Let's grow up.

Girls have a responsibility at this point too. Women, be

extremely honest in your response when a man declares his intentions to you. In some cases, that honesty may demand declining the offer to move beyond friendship. But if you've gotten the same green lights in your life, honesty might mean saying, "I'm ready to test and be tested!" It's a two-way street. The guy works to win your affections, but you're on trial as well. Are you ready to let this special man closer to your heart and to be tested by his family?

These are big questions, aren't they? But we need to ask and answer them to escape the limbo of directionless, inappropriately intimate relationships.

5. *Honor her parents.*

In Jason's case, Shelly was actually the second person to find out about his desire to pursue marriage. After an extended time of getting to know her and praying, Jason felt confident enough to move forward. But before he went into action, he chose to give proper honor to Shelly's parents, first by asking their permission to grow closer to their daughter for the purpose of pursuing marriage.

Personally, I intend to do the same thing. In my mind, this is the best way to start off your relationship with your potential in-laws. I know this won't always be possible. Some guys I know have asked the girl first and then have gone to her parents. In other situations, a father or mother isn't close by or active in this aspect of parenthood. Whatever the case, the principle is important: A young man ought to show respect for the person responsible for the girl. If that means approaching her pastor or grandfather, do it. If it means writing, calling, or e-mailing her folks on the other side of the world, do that. Go the distance to give them the respect they deserve.

Put Yourself on Trial

At this point, invite the girl's parents to ask pointed questions. What kind of plan do you have to support their daughter? What kind of activities will you pursue as you attempt to win her hand in marriage? The parents' questions will vary, depending on their relationship with their daughter and their personal convictions. Unfortunately, many parents won't really care. They may think you're being melodramatic or taking things too seriously. "Hey, if you want to take out our daughter, go for it." But many will be excited to participate in advising and counseling you during this exciting stage of the relationship.

A girl's parents may have specific concerns about the relationship or the timing of the relationship. One father I know questioned the spiritual maturity of a young man who was interested in his daughter. This young man had only recently come back to the Lord and had broken off an engagement with another girl four months earlier. The dad asked the young man to back off and prove himself over the next few months. The young guy proved himself, but not in the right way. He refused to honor the father's request and kept trying to see the girl behind her parents' backs. Finally, the girl told him that she wasn't interested in pursuing a deeper relationship with him.

No matter what response you receive from the parents, be humble enough to listen and honor them. God will bless you for doing so. Remember, they've invested a big part of their lives in their daughter. And God has placed them in her life to protect her. Don't try to circumvent their authority. Instead, work with it and benefit from their wisdom.

6. *Test and build the relationship in real-life settings.*

Now the relationship moves into a very exciting stage that's been lost in our current pattern for relationships. This is the time for the young man to win the girl's heart and for the two of them to test the wisdom of their potential marriage. It's a time of growing intimacy, but unlike the intimacy in many dating relationships, this intimacy has a purpose.

We want to insert a transitional stage between deepening friendship and engagement—a period of "principled romance." This is not simply for the sake of having romantic fun. Principled romance is purposeful in its pursuit of marriage, protected in its avoidance of sexual temptation, and account-able to parents or other Christians.

This time has distinct objectives and responsibilities. During the heart-winning/testing stage of their relationship, my friends Jeff and Danielle Myers looked for activities that allowed them to serve others and learn together. Though they did some things alone as a couple, they spent the majority of their time together with family and friends. They'd go on double dates with their parents and cook dinner for different married couples in the church.

Bringing Romance Home

One of the most unfortunate aspects of contemporary dating is the way it has removed the process of romance from the warmth and reality of the home. So much of dating separates two people from the people who know and love them best instead of fusing their two families together. Later in marriage a couple will value the support and involvement of both sides of the family. Now is the time to strengthen those relationships.

Parents' support and guidance during this time, when avail-able, is invaluable. One family wrote the following guidelines to help their daughter and her suitor. Although these guidelines were written for a specific couple with specific circumstances, I think you'll find them helpful in clarifying the purpose and focus of this stage.

1. Winston is to build Melody's trust.

2. Begin building an intimate relationship. Talk about many subjects. Discuss feelings, concerns, visions, hopes, dreams. Learn each other's basic convictions.

3. Attempt to understand each other: the differences between men and women, goals and roles, how each other thinks and responds to life.

4. Attempt to understand what things each values and detests.

5. Begin investing in each other by praying for each other, serving each other, gifting each other. Examples: Letters, phone calls, flowers.

6. Spend time together mostly in the family circle but also in short alone times—walks together, sitting in the swing together. Please avoid a "dating mentality." This is a learning and communicating time.

Even if you don't have the involvement of your parents, these kinds of guidelines can help you pursue a principled relationship. These guidelines wisely allow love to unfold and protect the process by keeping interaction within safe boundaries. Find creative ways in your own relationship to keep the focus on learning, testing, and growth, not just reveling in romantic love. This will allow you to truly get to know each other and make the wisest possible choice concerning marriage.

Ready for Forever

The period of testing and winning the heart need last only as long as it takes for both to feel confident about getting married. The moment comes when the time for observing, praying, thinking, and talking is over. Then it's time to "pop the question," as they say (stage 4). By this time, it should come as no surprise, yet it's still a moment to make special.

Obviously if, during the stage of testing, problems and concerns arise regarding the wisdom of the union, you should halt the relationship's progress or even consider calling it off. But if both of you are confident of your love for each other, and both sets of parents support your relationship, you have no reason to delay getting engaged and planning your wedding.

7. *Reserve passion for marriage.*

Finally, throughout your God-honoring relationship, set clear guidelines for physical affection. Here I can only reiterate what we discussed in chapter 6: Purity is a direction, not a line we suddenly cross by "going too far." The enemy of your soul would love to mar the beauty of your blossoming love by leading you down a path of lust and sexual compromise. Please don't give him a foothold.

I like Elisabeth Elliot's advice to couples: "Keep your hands off and your clothes on." Until you're married, please don't treat each other as if your bodies belong to each other. The kissing, touching, and caressing that take place in today's dating relationships often lead to confusion and compromise. Such behavior is often based on selfishness and awakens desires that you can righteously satisfy only in marriage. Protect each other and reserve your passion for marriage by refusing to start the process.

Personally, I've committed to waiting, even for a kiss, until I'm married. I want the first kiss with my wife to be on our wedding day. I know that sounds archaic to many, and truthfully, I would have scoffed at the idea myself four years ago. But I've come to realize how sinful and meaningless physical intimacy can be apart from the commitment and purity of marriage.

Focus on the Soul

Holding off the physical side of the relationship, though difficult, will enable you to focus on the soul of your spouse-to-be. A couple once told me their motto was, "Where physical progression begins, depth progression ends." In other words, as soon as they began to focus on the physical side of their relationship, the spiritual and emotional side ceased to deepen. Make a commitment to God, parents, Christian mentors, friends, and your partner to let your passion sleep, storing up your desire for the marriage bed. It will awaken with joy at the proper time.

Part of keeping this kind of commitment involves avoiding settings given to temptation. This doesn't mean you can never have privacy. But two people can have privacy and time alone without completely isolating themselves from parents and friends. When you do have activities that involve just the two of you, make sure you carefully plan your time, avoid a sensual focus and atmosphere, and let someone know where you'll be and when you'll be home.

Remember, by delaying sexual involvement, you're storing up passion and making sexual love within your marriage that much more meaningful. Don't allow impatience now to rob you of an undefiled, passionate sexual relationship in marriage.

Guided by the Holy Spirit

The new pattern we've discussed is only an outline. As with anything, a couple can manipulate it to fulfill only the minimum requirements. But I believe such manipulation will rob a couple of experiencing God's best. "But when the Holy Spirit controls our lives," the Bible tells us, "he will produce this kind of fruit in us: love, joy, peace, patience, kindness, goodness, faithfulness, gentleness, and self-control" (Galatians 5:22–23, NLT).

When the Holy Spirit guides our journey toward marriage, our relationships will exhibit the same qualities.

The progression from *casual friendship* to *deeper friendship* to *purposeful intimacy with integrity* to *engagement* won't solve the world's relational problems. (As long as sinners like you and me are involved, we can always find a way to mess things up!) But it can move us toward a safer, wiser approach to marriage. And for those truly committed to pleasing God and loving others sincerely, I hope this new pattern can bring a much needed renewal of purity, boldness, and true romance to modern love stories. I encourage you to create your own one-of-a-kind love story by following God-honoring principles for relationships. You'll never regret seeking His best for you and your mate-to-be!

CHAPTER SIXTEEN

Someday I'll Have a Story to Tell

WRITING A LOVE STORY YOU'LL FEEL PROUD TO TELL

Nothing is quite as romantic as hearing an honest, unabridged account of a married couple's love story. And you are quite privileged when you can hear this story from your parents.

I grew up hearing how my parents met and married. Polaroids from family photo albums serve as visual aids helping me "see" Mom and Dad as they were when they caught each other's eye. In my mind, I step back through time, silently observing their moment of destiny...

Dayton, Ohio, is an unlikely setting for a stirring romance. Dad likes to point out that Dayton was the birthplace of both the airplane and the self-starting car engine—devices, he jokes, to help you get out of town fast. But, despite my father's humorous sentiments, in 1973 this town served as the stage for my parents' love story.

As I "time travel" to 1973, I decide to visit the church my parents both attend. First Baptist Church sits on the corner of Maple and Ridgeway Street, a mix of old tradition and the young, sometimes unruly group of "Jesus people" of which my parents are a part. I find a seat at the coffeehouse located in the basement of an old house next to the church. "The Rock," as they call it, is full of high school and college students. A young man in faded jeans and a T-shirt sits on a stool in the corner of the room, playing guitar and singing. He's my father.

His hair is long and scraggly. I can't help but smile at how skinny he is. Of course he has his mustache. "Some things never change," I think to myself.

The song he sings is simple but passionate. "Three chords and the truth," he'll call it some day in the future. I've heard this song before but by an older man who sang it for the sake of nostalgia, frequently breaking to ask, "Now how did that line go?" Here, played by someone my age, it grips me.

Time's coming, and it won't be long.
Everybody's going to be gone.
We're going to meet at the Great White Throne;
Some are going to wonder what's going on.

I had forgotten that as a young man my dad faced an unknown and confusing world too. At this point in his life, he has only recently returned to the Lord and to his hometown of Dayton. For the last several years, he has moved from resort to resort—Laguna Beach, Lake Tahoe, Vail—playing his guitar and singing for tips in restaurants. Now the one-time hitchhiking runaway plays his guitar for Jesus. Many wonder if he'll ever amount to anything. (He will.)

My mom is here tonight too. What a strange thing to see my mother as a beautiful young girl. I can't take my eyes off her. She has all the mannerisms as a young woman that I've observed in her throughout my life. She's so different and yet so much the same. Is it any wonder Dad grew to love her? I see her give my dad a quick glance while he plays. She's trying not to seem too impressed.

At this point in her life, Mom has been a Christian for only a year. She's still a bit headstrong and independent. At nineteen, she's a talented ballet dancer whose conversion to Christ has disrupted her ambitions for a professional career. Uncertain of her future, she's leaning toward the possibility of foreign missions. Of some things she is sure: She never wants to marry, and she never, *ever* wants to have children. I wonder how she'd respond if I introduced myself to her as the first of her six kids.

I steal closer to her table when I notice my dad walking over. I don't want to miss their conversation. Dad tries to appear aimless as he wanders in her direction, but he obviously wants to talk to her.

"He never was very subtle," I say quietly. I'm near enough to hear as he approaches and greets her.

"Hey, Sono, I was wondering if you and your sister need a ride home."

"So *this* is the night!" I think to myself. I've heard the story of this conversation countless times. I lean forward to hear my mom's reply.

"No, thanks," she says. "Newton Tucker is driving us home."

My mom can be curt when she wants to, and tonight she's in full form. Completely unconcerned, she barely attempts to be polite.

"Well...maybe I can give you a call sometime," my dad says.

"Thank goodness he's so clueless," I think to myself. "Any other guy would take a hint and give up. But not Dad. No, siree! And it's a good thing, too. If it weren't for that indomitable Harris spirit, I wouldn't be here!"

My mom looks up at him again and gives a noncommittal "Mmm-hmm," obviously inconvenienced.

"Uh, what's your phone number?" he asks as she stands up to go.

She looks at him, pauses momentarily, then says, "It's in the church directory."

"Ouch!" I say out loud. "Mom can be so cold. 'It's in the directory.' Now *that* is harsh."

My dad stands silently as she walks away, and he sighs as she disappears up the steps. The situation looks pretty hopeless.

But then, I know the end of the story, and it's my favorite part. This is where God gets involved.

That night, after the infamous "It's in the directory" speech, my mom and dad prayed about each other in the privacy of their two bedrooms.

My mom's iciness toward the guitar-playing boy at the coffeehouse was not without explanation. She enjoyed his music, and his seriousness about the Lord had caught her attention. But since coming to the Lord, she had been hounded by girl-crazy Christian guys whose faith hadn't done much to reign in their hormones. More than one had told her that God had spoken to him and said she would marry him. My mom quickly learned that many guys would use religious overtures just to get the girl. She was fed up and disgusted.

"Lord," she prayed, "if this guy is different from all the rest, if he really listens to you, than tell him not to call me." She turned off her bedroom light and went to sleep.

On the other side of town, my dad said his own prayer. A fair share of false starts with girls had left him unsure of what he should do. "God, please show me if I should call this girl." The prayer was more a matter of form than an actual request; God had never before intervened in his romantic interests, and Dad didn't expect Him to do so this time either. In fact, he was already planning to call and was even forming a speech that he hoped would sweep Mom off her feet.

But that night Dad encountered something different. He clearly sensed God speaking to him. "Gregg, don't call her."

God had spoken. My dad obeyed.

The rest, as they say, is history.

Confusing and Messy

Though it's hard to imagine, someday I'll tell *my* children the story I'm writing with my life today. But that realization does little to save me from the puzzling maze called now. "History never looks like history when you're living through it," says John Gardner. "It always looks confusing and messy, and it always feels uncomfortable."

As I stand on this side of matrimony with no potential mate in sight, I'm right in the middle of the messiness and confusion. I still have so many questions. Will I know when I'm walking through the story for the first time? Will I recognize the event that will begin the chapters of my love story with my mate?

Will time stand still for one moment to tell me that this person—this one person, out of all the billions bustling on the planet—is *the one?* Will I realize when it happens? Or might I miss it?

Some questions are probably best left unasked. I know I should push them aside and wait for life to unfold its mysteries. Someday when I'm older and wiser I'll sit back and tell my story to someone who will listen. And as I tell my story, will I remember the doubts and questioning prayers of today? Or will I have forgotten the silent longings; will they wash away like footprints on an ocean shore? I'll probably tell some young fool the same things I get so tired of hearing from others. I'll tell him to bide his time, "for it's sure to work out in the end." And, of course, "you can't rush these things."

Someday I'll have a story to tell. So will you. How will you respond when one day you look back on your love story? Will it bring tears of joy or tears of remorse? Will it remind you of God's goodness or your lack of faith in that goodness? Will it be a story of purity, faith, and selfless love? Or will it be a story of impatience, selfishness, and compromise? It's your choice.

I encourage you (and continue to remind myself) to write a love story with your life that you'll feel proud to tell.

Notes

CHAPTER 2

Stephen Olford—Stephen Olford, "Social Relationships," a sermon recorded at Moody Bible Institute.

C. S. Lewis—C. S. Lewis, *The Four Loves* (Orlando, Fla.: Harcourt Brace and Company, 1960), 66.

Elisabeth Elliot—Elisabeth Elliot, *Passion and Purity* (Grand Rapids, Mich.: Baker Book House, 1984), 153.

CHAPTER 5

William J. Bennett—William J. Bennett, *The Book of Virtues* (New York: Simon and Schuster, 1993), 57.

Marshmallows—Nancy Gibbs, "The EQ Factor," *Time* (October 2, 1995), 60.

Elisabeth Elliot—Elisabeth Elliot, *Passion and Purity*, 164.

John Fischer—John Fischer, "A Single Person's Identity," a sermon delivered August 5, 1973, at Peninsula Bible Church, Palo Alto, Calif.

May Riley Smith—May Riley Smith, "Sometime," *The Best Loved Poems of the American People* (New York: Doubleday and Company, 1936), 299.

CHAPTER 6

"Recognize the Deep Significance of Physical Intimacy"—I am indebted to Lynn Denby, who wrote me a letter and challenged my thinking about how guys and girls should relate before marriage.

Billy Graham—William Martin, *A Prophet with Honor: The Billy Graham Story* (New York: William Morrow and Company, 1991), 107.

CHAPTER 7

The Room—Joshua Harris, "The Room," *New Attitude* (Spring 1995), 31. Reprinted with permission.

CHAPTER 9

C. S. Lewis—C. S. Lewis, *The Four Loves*, 66.

CHAPTER 10

Elisabeth Elliot—Elisabeth Elliot, *Passion and Purity*, 31.

Stephen Covey—Stephen Covey, A. Roger Merrill, and Rebecca R. Merrill, *First Things First* (New York: Simon and Schuster, 1994).

Beilby Porteus—Dr. Ruth C. Haycock, ed. *The Encyclopedia of Bible Truths for School Subjects* (Association of Christian Schools, 1993), 393.

CHAPTER 12

Catherine Vos—Catherine F. Vos, *The Child's Story Bible* (Grand Rapids, Mich.: William B. Eerdmans Publishing Company), 29. Used with permission.

Gregg Harris—Gregg Harris, "The Adventure of Current Obligations," *The Family Restoration Quarterly* 1 (February 1987), 2.

CHAPTER 13

Ricucci—Gary Ricucci and Betsy Ricucci, *Love that Lasts: Making a Magnificent Marriage* (Gaithersburg, Md.: People of Destiny, 1992), 7–10. Used with permission.

Mike Mason—Mike Mason, *The Mystery of Marriage: As Iron Sharpens Iron* (Sisters, Ore.: Multnomah Books, 1985), 166.

Ann Landers—Ann Landers, "All Marriages Are Happy." Permission granted by Ann Landers and Creators Syndicate.

Lena Lathrop—Lena Lathrop, "A Woman's Question," *The Best Loved Poems of the American People*, 22.

CHAPTER 14

Randy Alcorn—Randy Alcorn, "O. J. Simpson: What Can We Learn?", *Eternal Perspectives* (Summer 1994).

William Davis—William Davis, "Reputation and Character," *The Treasure Chest: Memorable Words of Wisdom and Inspiration* (San Francisco: Harper Collins, 1995), 54.

Samuel Smiles—William Thayer, *Gaining Favor with God and Man* (San Antonio: Mantle Ministries, 1989), 41.

David Powlison and John Yenchko—David Powlison and John Yenchko, "Should We Get Married?" *Journal of Biblical Counseling* 14, (Spring 1996), 42.

A. W. Tozer—A. W. Tozer, *The Best of AW Tozer* (Grand Rapids, Mich.: Baker Book House, 1978), 111.

Bill Bennett—William J. Bennett, *The Book of Virtues*, 347.

E. V. Hill—James Dobson, *Focus on the Family Newsletter* (February 1995), 3.

Charlotte Mason—Charlotte M. Mason, *The Original Homeschooling Series* 1 (Wheaton, Ill.: Tyndale House Publishers, 1989).

Benjamin Tillett—*The Encyclopedia of Religious Quotations* (Westwood, N.J.: Fleming H. Revell Co., 1965), 298.

Benjamin Franklin—*Notable Quotables* (Chicago: World Book Encyclopedia, 1984), 65.

CHAPTER 15

Wycliffe—Charles F. Pfeiffer, ed. *Wycliffe Bible Commentary* (Chicago: Moody Press, 1962), 603.

"Guidelines for Winston and Melody"—Kenneth and Julie McKim, *Family Heritage Newsletter* (September 1994).

Elisabeth Elliot—Elisabeth Elliot, *Quest for Love* (Grand Rapids, Mich.: Baker Book House, 1996), 269.

CHAPTER 16

John Gardner—*Notable Quotables*, 48.

Dad's Song—Gregg Harris, "It's a Shame," © 1972.

Thanks...

To Apple Computers for the Duo 230.

To Don Miller for dreaming with me over dinners of "spit roast, chili-rubbed chicken."

To Greg Somerville and Donna Partow, who told me to go for it.

To Randy Alcorn, who showed me kindness when I could do nothing for him in return. He advised me about book proposals, introduced me to Questar Publishers, and offered counsel and encouragement during writing. To Karina Alcorn for reading the first chapters.

To Stephanie Storey, who demanded that "someone read this kid's proposal." To Brenda Saltzer for reading it. To Don Jacobson and Questar for believing that nobodies can write books too. To Dan Benson for shepherding, and to Lisa Lauffer for editing. To everyone else at Questar who strives for excellence. I am so honored to be on this team.

To Michael Farris for "believing in what is unseen."

To Gary and Betsy Ricucci for providing insight about marriage. To John Loftness for impromptu editing.

To all the *New Attitude* magazine readers and conference attendees who prayed for and believed in this project. To those who wrote and shared from their lives: Grace Ludlum, Anna Soennecken, and the "Eugene Harris" pen pals in particular.

To Amy Walsh, Greg Spencer, Kay Lindly, Debbie Lechner, Matt and Jennie Chancey, Amy Brown, Martha Rupert, Matt and Julie Canlis, Sarah Schlissel, Rebekah Garfield, Kristine Banker, Rebecca Livermore, and Josh Carden, who listened to my ideas and shared their invaluable perspective at just the right time.

To "the gang," my brothers and sisters in the Lord: Ben Trolese, Ruth and Sheena Littlehale, Julie Womack, and Sharon Stricker, whose encouragement, friendship, and example were a beacon of hope during the manuscript's final stages. Thanks for enduring the conversations: "Do we have to talk about love and romance again?" Thanks for being real. I spoke from my heart because of you.

To Grandma Sato who has talked me through more than one "girl problem."

To Rebecca St. James for writing the foreword, but more important, for friendship and exuberance about serving God.

To Mrs. Elliot Gren for a lifetime of faithfulness to our Lord.

To Andrew Garfield, my accountability partner and brother, whose service at the conferences allowed me to give myself to writing. The next hot dog at O'Hare is on me, bro.

To my brother Joel, who let me leave the light on at night while I wrote.

To my other siblings, Alex, Brett, Sarah, and Isaac, without whom I could have finished this book long ago. I'd have it no other way—thanks for the noise.

To C. J. Mahaney for defending the doctrine of sin and the Church. Thanks for the hours on the phone "adjusting."

To Janet Albers, my second mom and a true "co-laborer" in Christ. She managed New Attitude magazine while I was writing this book. She proofed; she edited; she did it all. Thanks for believing in me.

To my mom and dad, who were, and always will be, my first editors. Thanks for raising me to shoot for the stars. Thank you for nursing me through writer's block and rejoicing with me over every finished chapter. My triumph is your triumph. My victory is yours. I love you.

To Jesus Christ, "the giver of the gift, the blesser of the action, the aid of the project." He orchestrated and guided. He gave me all of these people. He forgave me. Thank you, Lord!

About the Author

Joshua Harris hasn't lived long enough to have much of a bio, but he's working on that. For four years he published and edited *New Attitude,* the Christian magazine for home-school teens. He closed the magazine at the end of 1996 to move from his hometown of Portland, Oregon, to the east coast, where he's currently receiving training and discipleship from the pastors at Covenant Life Church in Gaithersburg, Maryland. He desires to serve and bless the body of Christ through the local church; when he grows up, he wants to be a pastor.

In the meantime, Joshua also speaks nationally at *New Attitude* conferences and other events. For a current listing of these events, visit the *New Attitude* website at:

http://www.newattitude.com/~joshuah/

To contact Josh regarding speaking and other matters, write to him at the following addresses (he loves to get mail, and he welcomes your feedback on this book):

Joshua Harris
P.O. Box 249
Gaithersburg, MD 20884-0249
E-mail: DOIT4JESUS@AOL.COM